Extroversion/Introversion
in Foreign Language Learning

D1732775

Linguistic Insights

Studies in Language and Communication

Edited by Maurizio Gotti,
University of Bergamo

Volume 67

PETER LANG
Bern · Berlin · Bruxelles · Frankfurt am Main · New York · Oxford · Wien

Natsumi Wakamoto

Extroversion/Introversion in Foreign Language Learning

Interactions with Learner Strategy Use

PETER LANG
Bern · Berlin · Bruxelles · Frankfurt am Main · New York · Oxford · Wien

Bibliographic information published by Die Deutsche Bibliothek
Die Deutsche Bibliothek lists this publication in the Deutsche National-
bibliografie; detailed bibliographic data is available on the Internet at
‹http://dnb.ddb.de›.

British Library and Library of Congress Cataloguing-in-Publication Data:
A catalogue record for this book is available from *The British Library,*
Great Britain.

Library of Congress Cataloging-in-Publication Data

Wakamoto, Natsumi.
Extroversion/introversion in foreign language learning :
interactions with learner strategy use / Natsumi Wakamoto.
p. cm. – (Linguistic insights ; v. 67) (Studies in language and communication)
Includes bibliographical references and index.
ISBN 978-3-03911-596-9 (alk. paper)
1. Languages, Modern–Study and teaching (Higher)–Japan. 2. English language–
Study and teaching (Higher)–Japanese speakers. 3. Second language
acquisition–Japan–Psychological aspects. 4. Personality–Japan. 5. Language
and emotions. I. Title.
PB38.J3W35 2009
418.0071'152–dc22

2009007260

ISSN 1424-8689
ISBN 978-3-03911-596-9

© Peter Lang AG, International Academic Publishers, Bern 2009
Hochfeldstrasse 32, Postfach 746, CH-3000 Bern 9, Switzerland
info@peterlang.com, www.peterlang.com, www.peterlang.net

Printed in Germany

To my parents
with love and gratitude

Contents

Preface

This book is a revised version of my doctoral dissertation submitted to Ontario Institute for Studies in Education of the University of Toronto (OISE/UT), Canada, titled *The impact of extroversion/introversion and associated learner strategies on English language comprehension in a Japanese EFL setting.* Looking back, working on my dissertation was a splendid and unforgettable journey, in every aspect of which I was able to meet wonderful people, without whose help I could not have completed this book. My gratitude extends foremost to my dissertation supervisor, Sharon Lapkin, for her constant encouragement, valuable comments, and suggestions throughout every stage of this project, and to my thesis committee members, Merrill Swain and Nina Spada, for their careful reading, incisive feedback, and valuable suggestions. I am thankful to Alister Cumming, Shizuhiko Nishisato, Sue Elgie, and other instructors of courses I took at OISE/UT, from whom I learned the requirements and procedures of second/foreign language learning research. I thank Rebecca Oxford, who granted me permission to include her strategy questionnaire in this book. Her work provided the trigger for my research about learner strategies and by acting as my external examiner, she also helped me complete my work. The research of Jean-Mark Dewaele and Vivien Berry provided further impetus for my work.

My deep appreciation goes also to my colleague, Barbara Fujiwara, who encouraged me from the beginning to the end, helping me through the rough times in Japan. She always read my drafts with her marvelously patient attention. I also acknowledge and thank Tim Medlock and the students of Doshisha Women's College who participated in my study. I am very grateful for the support from my colleagues and friends in Japan, who constantly gave me warm encouragement and comments on my drafts. Among others, I wish to thank Yasuyo Edasawa, Tsuyoshi Iida, Shuhei Kadota, Misaki Kitajima, Kathleen Kitao, Toshihisa Koizumi, Hiroshi Mine, Manabu Murase, Toshiyo Nabei, Kazuko Nakajima, Judy Noguchi, Yukinobu Oda, Namie Saeki, Kiyone

Sakamoto, Hitomi Sugihara, Bernard Susser, Hideyuki Takashima, Osamu Takeuchi, Nicholas Teele, and Charley Thorp. My appreciation also goes to my students, especially my seminar students at Doshisha Women's College from 1997 through 2008. Through discussions with them, I obtained the inspiration for my research.

I thank my friends in Toronto: Jane Freeman and Robert Luke for their splendid English writing support when I met difficulties; Bernadette and Christian for good mutual support with our comprehensive exams; Samantha and Dorothy for various co-presentations; and all the others at the Modern Language Centre of OISE/UT. I have especially good memories of the pleasant times Joshua Haglund and I shared; I remain deeply saddened by his death. I am grateful to the Hirata, Matsubayashi and Young families, who always welcomed me when I returned to Toronto. I also cannot forget the kindness of William and Hiroko Keith, who provided insight, delicious food, and a place to stay.

I thank Maurizio Gotti, editor of this series, for his kind offer of publishing this book and detailed suggestions to improve the draft, and Ursula Rettinghaus for her kind assistance as well. I also thank Doshisha Women's College of Liberal Arts for granting me a sabbatical, during which time I could begin the research for this dissertation, and for providing the financial support to publish this book.

Last, but not least, I thank my devoted wife, Kuniko, my dearest son, Atsushi, and my dearest daughter, Yachiyo. Even in difficult times, they were always with me and cheered me up. I can easily imagine how difficult it was for them to adjust to the new environment of Toronto, but they never complained. I could not have pursued the Ed.D. program at OISE/UT without their sincere love and strong support.

This is the first book that I have published in my life, and I dedicate this book to my parents, Mitsuharu and Junko, who provided me with a good education and guided me in the right direction with their honest and insightful words derived from their belief in God. They have had a profound influence on my life and on my thinking. They have given me more than I can say.

Natsumi Wakamoto
January 12, 2009, Kyoto, Japan

1.   Introduction

1.1.   Rationale for the study

The importance of learning second/foreign languages differs from country to country and from person to person. For Japanese people, learning English has been a great concern for a long time, at least for the last decades. Young parents would like to have their children attend English conversation or 'cram' schools (*juku*) – i.e., supplemental private for-profit schools – from an early age. There are a number of English language programs on television as well as commercial English conversation schools even in small towns. Since 1987, the Ministry of Education, Culture, Sports, Science, and Technology (MEXT) has invited up to 5,000 native speakers of English from various English-speaking countries every year to introduce authentic English into the classrooms of junior or senior high schools. However, English has often cast a dark shadow on Japanese people's minds. This is because learning English has been a struggle for them in spite of their enthusiasm for learning English. Many people have felt that it is unfair to have to devote so much time to learning English when people who happened to be born in English-speaking countries do not have to make such an effort.

The broad topics I will explore in my volume are the language learning difficulties common to Japanese learners of English, and the individual differences among them. The common problems can be expressed in the following way: Why does learning English in Japan entail such great difficulty? This is a question that many Japanese people are curious about; they ask themselves why they do not have even the ability to make simple daily conversation despite having studied English for six years or more. At the same time, it is also true that second/foreign language learners learn differently, even if they are learning under the same conditions and experience the same teaching methods in the same classroom. This issue calls to mind Cook's (2002: 219) classic question:

"why some people pick up second languages quickly and easily, and others never become fluent up to their dying day." This question is significant for both teachers and learners. In fact, my interest in research in this field developed out of my ten years' experience as a public junior high school teacher in Japan. I could not help wondering what were the barriers that impeded learners' progress in English, and why learners in similar learning environments differed in their levels of language proficiency and in their levels of motivation for learning English.

With respect to individual differences, I will focus on learners' personality types, specifically extroversion and introversion (henceforth, E/I), because it is my hypothesis that personality type is a key factor for Japanese people learning English in Japan. To investigate the impact of E/I, I will pay attention to the influence of E/I on learner strategies use as well as listening proficiency as one skill area for which standardized test data are available.

1.2. Overview of the volume

I will initiate my discussion by reviewing the research literature of individual differences in relation to E/I and learner strategies. Chapter 2 presents a literature review of learner strategy research and of the relationship between personality type and foreign/second language learning, and specifies the research questions of this study. Chapter 3 describes the research methods used in this study in the following way: Phase I, which is based on a questionnaire data; Phase II on classroom observation data; and Phase III on observations in individual learning conditions. Chapter 4 presents the results of this study, and in Chapter 5, I will discuss the findings, phase by phase. Finally, Chapter 6 provides the conclusions of this study, and a statement of its implications for further research.

2. Literature Review

2.1. Historical overview of research on individual differences

From the late 1960s through the early 1970s, part of the foci of language teaching research shifted from teaching methods to the learners themselves and their learning processes. Stern (1983: 110) supported this claim in the following description: "the disillusionment over the teaching method debate and the inconclusiveness of the method research prompted a number of theorists to demand a search for a deeper understanding of the nature of the second language learning process itself." A concern arose with regard to how learners engage in their learning tasks in a second or foreign language. This prompted the beginning of second language acquisition (henceforth, SLA) research in this area. One research emphasis has been directed towards exploring the similarities among learners – especially towards investigating what processes of learning are common or universal, as indicated by studies of Universal Grammar (e.g., Chomsky 1959; Pinker 1994), error analysis (e.g., Corder 1967; Dulay/Burt 1973), morpheme studies or studies on the developmental stages of negation or interrogation (e.g., Dulay/Burt 1974; Schumann 1979; Wode 1977). In the mid-1970s, however, a further concern for the differences among learners as articulated in the Good Language Learner study (Naiman/Fröhlich/Stern/Todesco 1978/1996) came to the attention of EFL (English as a foreign language) researchers, which proved seminal in the research on individual differences. One reason for this may have been the following observation from studies comparing teaching methodologies: "learners who benefit from a particular methodology are canceled out by those for whom it is inappropriate" (Skehan 1991: 295). The failure of such studies can be attributed to the fact that they "lumped all learners together" (Skehan 1991: 295). This analysis supports the idea that it is important to pay attention to individual learners themselves, and in particular to note their characteristics, because learners do not start from a blank slate. Rather, learners enter the learning process with their own predispositions and ways of learning a language, including their own learning strategies.

Such research interest in the individual differences (ID) among learners corresponds to classroom teachers' simple question: Why are some learners more successful than others even if they are learning under the same conditions and experiencing the same teaching methods in the same classroom? This question on the remarkable differences of achievement among learners has become one of mounting concern for English teachers in Japan, because students have been losing interest in English lessons, and an increasing number are opting out of English lessons at the higher levels (Takanashi/Takahashi 1990). This phenomenon continues to occur, despite teachers' efforts to improve their teaching methods. Teachers are asking themselves whether it is in fact possible to guide less effective learners to success through English education. Knowing how language learners actually learn will help EFL teachers in Japan develop more effective teaching methods. Questions that pre-occupy educators include:

a) what factors influence student success in learning English?

b) what are the decisive elements that separate more effective and less effective learners?

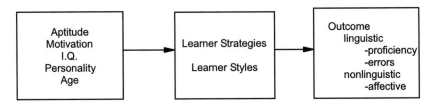

Figure 1. Influences of language learning (Skehan 1991: 277).

Skehan's (1991) model of individual differences clarifies the relationship among factors influencing individual differences and underlines the pivotal role of learner strategies and styles. In this model, the factors listed in the box on the left are naturally endowed (aptitude, I.Q., personality) or unchangeable (age), except for motivation.

16

Learner strategies and learning styles, in an intermediate position between the left-box (individual learner characteristics) and right-box variables (outcomes), play a significant role in mediating the influences of the left-box variables on learning outcomes. Learning styles can be distinguished from strategies in that they are consistent and rather enduring tendencies (Brown 2000). Learner strategies are a curious factor as their nature is flexible, corresponding to learners' left-box variables as well as task types. Examining learners' strategy use reveals the characteristics of each learner's language learning, and teachers are able to know more about how learners are learning foreign languages. Teachers may also attempt to provide less successful learners with effective strategies used by successful learners because learners' proficiency will improve through using those effective strategies.

Numerous and important studies have been conducted on variables listed in the left-box (e.g., Gardner 2000; Patkowski 1980; Robinson 2002; Snow/Hoefnagel-Höhle 1978), but there has not been much research on personality until recently (Dewaele/Furnham 1999). It is believed that E/I are significant predictors for success in learning foreign languages for Japanese people (Griffiths 1991; Muranoi/ Chiba/Hatanaka 2002). By combining research on E/I and learner strategies, we can expect to find a different perspective on foreign language learning. In the following sections, I will outline the relevant previous studies on E/I in relation to foreign language learning.

2.2. Extroversion/introversion and language learning

2.2.1. Definition of extroversion/introversion

The terms 'extrovert' and 'introvert' were first used and developed by Carl Gustav Jung as part of his type theories (Jung 1987); since then, E/I has become a widely and generally acknowledged and used personality construct.

E/I has been investigated broadly from two perspectives: the biological and the social. From a biological point of view, E/I can be discussed in relation to the arousal level in the cortex of the brain. Wilson and Languis (1990) confirmed Eysenck's predicttion (Eysenck 1947/1998) that extroverts are underaroused – less excited – and introverts are overaroused – over-excited in terms of cerebral activity. Underaroused people – extroverts (henceforth, Es) – inevitably seek more stimuli outside themselves, and their orientation of energy is toward the outer world. On the other hand, overaroused people – introverts (henceforth, Is) – do not need extra stimuli because they have sufficient internal stimuli, so their orientation of energy is toward an inner world (Figure 2). Thus, extroverts tend to "turn outward" and introverts tend to "turn inward" (Brown 2000; Myers 1998).

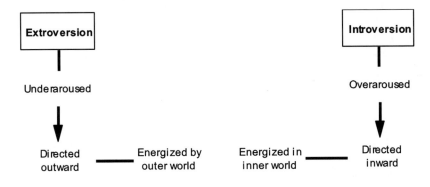

Figure 2. Orientation of energy (based on Myers 1998).

As a result, Es are energized by interaction with the outer world, people or things, and are active and outgoing, and they take the attitude of 'Live it, then understand it'. On the other hand, Is are energized by concentration on the inner world, thoughts and concepts, and are reflective and inwardly directed, and they take the attitude of 'Understand it, before living it' (Myers 1998; Myers/Kirby 1994; Myers/McCaulley/Quenk/Hammer 1998). Hofstede (1997) illustrates the relationship between biological and social influences on personality in the following way (Figure 3).

18

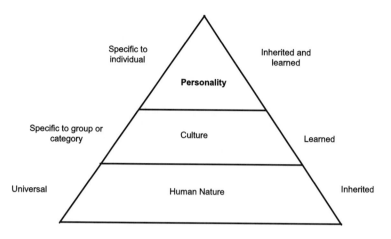

Figure 3. Three levels of uniqueness in human mental programming (Hofstede 1997: 6).

Figure 3 illustrates that personality is determined by the mixed influences of biological and socio-cultural influences. It stipulates that human nature is inherited and culture is nurtured. As a result, personality – E/I – is inherited as human nature and learned as culture. Because human nature is universal, the arousal level of extroverts (biological) should be the same among people of different backgrounds. On the other hand, culture is specific to groups of people and countries, and is therefore bound to influence personality. For example, Japanese people as a group are often assumed to be introverts. This is one typical example of cultural influences on personality, although to conclude that all the people in a cultural group are introverted or extroverted leads to the creation of stereotypes (Susser 1998a, 1998b). We can see from Figure 3 that we need to take account of both biological and socio-cultural influences when we examine people's E/I.

Theoretically, E/I has been researched under two important personality taxonomies – Big-Two Dimensions, consisting of Neuroticism and Extroversion (Eysenck 1947/1998; Eysenck/Eysenck 1985) and Big-Five, including Neuroticism, Extroversion, Agreeableness, Conscientiousness, and Openness to experience (Barbaranelli/Capara/ Rabasca/Pastorelli 2003; Gleitman/Fridlund/Reisberg 1999; McCrae/ Costa 2003). Although the two models differ in the number of categories, they "overlap considerably. [...] The Big Five construct retains Eysenck's first two dimensions" (Dörnyei 2005: 13); that is, extroversion appears in both models. Characteristics of typical extroverts and introverts are summarized in Table 1.

	Extroverts	*Introverts*
Sociability/ Interaction	like parties; need to have people to talk to	reserved and distant except to intimate friends
Excitement	crave excitement; act on the spur of the moment	do not like excitement; distrust the impulse of the moment
Expenditure of energies	carefree, easy-going, optimistic; like to 'laugh and be merry'; altogether their feelings are not kept under tight control	reliable, take matters of everyday life with proper seriousness, pessimistic; quiet, retiring sort of person, introspective
Risk-taking/ Planning	take chances; generally like change	plan ahead; 'look before they leap', like a well-ordered mode of life
Interest in external events	do not like reading or studying alone	fond of books rather than people

Table 1. Characteristic behaviors of extroverts and introverts (based on Eysenck/ Eysenck 1975).

As shown in Table 1, E/I is generally represented by the following adjectives: Extroverts are "sociable, gregarious, active, assertive, passionate, and talkative" and introverts are "passive, quiet, reserved, withdrawn, sober, aloof and restrained" (Dörnyei 2005: 15). These characteristics of Es and Is also correspond to those in Brown (2000), where he states that Es tend to be "willing to take conversational risks" and are "dependent on outside stimulation and interaction" whereas Is tend to have "concentration and self-sufficiency". Introverts' need to "process ideas before speaking sometimes led to avoidance of linguistic risks in conversation" (Brown 2000: 159).

2.2.2. Extroversion/introversion and language learning

Lightbown and Spada (1993, 1999, 2006) suggest that many classroom teachers are convinced that extroverts are more successful in second or foreign language learning than introverts, especially in terms of being superior in their communicative ability. In SLA research, however, extroversion has been the 'unloved' variable (Dewaele/Furnham 1999) and personality variables have tended to be omitted from the second language (L2) research agenda (Griffiths 1991); there have only been a limited number of research studies to date, and none has identified clearly the effects of extroversion or introversion on English proficiency (Dewaele/Furnham 1999).

Chastain (1975), for example, conducted a study to examine whether affective variables such as anxiety, creativity, and reserved vs. outgoing characteristics of students would have an influence on final course grades with college students in beginning French, German, and Spanish. His findings indicate that an outgoing personality (vs. reserved) was one of the factors positively and significantly related to course grades.

Swain and Burnaby (1976) investigated the relationship between personality characteristics and a number of second language learning performance measures of 131 school pupils such as vocabulary, comprehension, fluency, pronunciation and intonation as assessed by the French Comprehension Test, Test de Rendement en Français, and Test of Comprehension and Production, comparing those in a French immersion program and those in regular French as a second language (FSL) classes. The personality characteristics rated by their teachers included nine traits such as quickness in grasping new concepts, clinging to one's own opinions, happiness and cheerfulness, perfectionist tendencies, being sociable, being imaginative and creative, being independent, being anxious, and being talkative. As a result of this study, they found many significant correlations mainly in the French immersion pupils between the characteristics of quickness in grasping new concepts and perfectionist tendencies, and French learning achievement (1976: 123). Especially notable among those correlations is that concerning pronunciation, in which they found a negative correlation between pronunciation and quickness in grasping new

21

concepts ($r = -.35$, $p < .05$): "the quicker the child is to grasp new concepts the less likely he is to have native-like pronunciation in French" (1976: 123).

Swain and Burnaby's (1976) results were also confirmed by Busch's (1982) study in Japan. Busch (1982) examined the relationship between the extroversion and English proficiency of 185 Japanese learners of English in a junior college and a night school in Kobe, Japan. This study will be considered in detail because it concerns Japanese learners and offers some questions regarding E/I, gender-related 'role-behaviors', and language proficiency. Busch measured learners' extroversion using the Eysenck Personality Inventory (EPI), and English proficiency with a standardized English written test (YTEP, YMCA Test of English Proficiency) that consisted of sections on grammar and vocabulary, reading, aural comprehension, and dictation. In her study, she found no positive significant correlation between any sections of YTEP and extroversion. Instead, she found a weak negative correlation between extroversion and the sections of grammar/ vocabulary($r = -.18$, $p < .057$, n = 80) and reading ($r = -.16$, $p < .069$, n = 80). Furthermore, she examined the relationship between extroversion and oral proficiency because extroverts were assumed to be better than introverts in oral skills. She used an oral interview test that measured comprehension, pronunciation, fluency, and grammar. In her results, all the correlations that would indicate the relationship between extroversion and those subcomponents were negative though not significant. She found a significant negative correlation between extroversion and learners' pronunciation ($r = -.38$, $p < .009$, n = 39): introverts had better pronunciation than extroverts.

These results were contrary to her hypotheses and those of many people. The results were further examined by focusing on gender, which revealed a positive relationship between overall oral proficiency and extroversion only in male participants ($X^2 = 10.17$, $p < .04$, n = 17), not in females; however, caution was exercised in drawing conclusions because of the small male sample. This study provided me with invaluable insight into the influence of extroversion on language proficiency because it was conducted with Japanese participants who were learning English as a foreign language in Japan, and in addition examined the interaction between gender and extroversion. Busch offered gender-related 'role behavior' as an explanation as to why no positive relationship between oral proficiency and extroversion in females was found: "role behavior allows men to be more dominant and assertive, while women have to find a means of self-expression indirectly within the structure of the female role" (1982: 130). The explanation indicated the necessity of separating the role of gender when examining the influence of extroversion on English language learning; therefore, I decided to use only women participants in my study.

Strong (1983) tried to identify the influence of extroversion and other traits such as talkativeness or popularity on English learning. In his study, he could not find any significant relationship between extroversion and English oral proficiency. This might have been due to the fact that the number of participants was rather small (N = 13), or because his participants were kindergarten pupils. The Early School Personality Questionnaire (ESPQ) that was used to identify pupils' extroversion was perhaps "more about how a child would like to be, rather than how that child actually is" (1983: 256).

With first-year university students learning Spanish, Ely (1986) found that class risk-taking positively predicted classroom participation; he posited language class risk-taking and language class sociability as constructs related to extroversion-introversion, and learning language. His study indicates the importance of paying attention to students' behavior in the classroom.

Ehrman and Oxford (1990) found an important relationship between personality type and learner strategies in their study of 20 adults learning Turkish at the Foreign Service Institute in the U.S. As measurement tools, they used the Myers-Briggs Type Indicator (MBTI; see Section 3.2.2.1) for psychological type and the Strategy Inventory for Language Learning (SILL; see Section 3.2.2.3) and an interview for preferred language learning strategies. In addition to the influence of extroversion and introversion on the choice of strategies, they examined the influence of gender differences and the MBTI factors of Thinking/Feeling and Judging/Perceiving. By analyzing the interview results, they determined that extroverts preferred social strategies such as cooperation with others or asking for clarification, and functional practice strategies such as seeking practice opportunities outside of class. In contrast to extroverts, they discovered that introverts preferred to learn alone, and to avoid social contact and spontaneous situations.

In a larger-scale investigation with 855 American language learners of various languages such as Spanish or French, however, Ehrman and Oxford (1995) found no significant relations between E/I scores indicated by the MBTI and the Modern Language Aptitude Test scores.

Brown, Robson, and Rosenkjar (1996) conducted a large-scale study to examine personality, motivation, anxiety, strategies, and overall English proficiency measured by a cloze test and a grammar test with 320 Japanese university students in an intensive language program. Personality was measured with the Yatabe-Guilford (Y/G) Personality Inventory which identifies 12 personality traits including extroversion; it was translated into Japanese with 120 items. Their finding indicates that learning with others (social strategies) positively correlates with extroversion ($r = .31, p < .05$).

With the participation of EFL learners in Indonesia, Carrell, Prince, and Astika (1996) examined the relationship between personality types measured by the MBTI translated into an Indonesian language by the authors and language performance measures such as reading, writing, vocabulary, and grammatical tests. They found only a weak negative correlation between extroversion and vocabulary test scores ($r = -.19, p < .10$).

Hassan (2001) examined the relationship between extroversion-introversion and the pronunciation accuracy of English with 71 Arabic speaking third-year students learning English in an Egyptian university, and found a significantly positive correlation between English pronunciation accuracy and extroversion ($r = 25, p < .05$). We need to be cautious about the conclusion because males outperformed females on the pronunciation test and thus it is possible that it was gender that influenced the English pronunciation, since the result was opposite to that of Busch (1982). As a possible explanation, Hassan points out that extroverts are more fluent and accurate in the foreign language class because they are more sociable than introverts, who may be afraid of initiating interaction inside the class (Hassan 2001: 20).

The research literature on E/I shows mixed results, especially about the relationship between extroversion and English proficiency.

24

While a negative or weak correlation was reported in Swain/Burnaby (1976), Busch (1982), and Carrell/Prince/Astika (1996), a positive correlation was found in Chastain (1975) and Hassan (2001). No significant relationship was reported in Strong (1983) or Ehrman/Oxford (1995). This discrepancy might have been caused because different instruments were used to measure E/I, and as Berry (2004) points out, we need to recognize the importance of adopting an appropriate instrument to assess personality.

These mixed results point to the fact that extroversion has yet to be fully examined in the field of second language learning, and that the impacts of extroversion/introversion on language learning remain unclear or depend on other extra factors. Therefore, in view of the characteristics of Japanese classrooms, which will be discussed in Section 2.4.2, there arises the necessity to investigate the influence of extroversion and introversion in a solely Japanese context. In the next section, I will outline in what ways learner strategies can help address these concerns.

2.3. Learner strategies

2.3.1. Definitions

The term 'learner strategies' is sometimes used as a synonym for 'language learning strategies (LLSs)', and clear definitions of strategies have been a concern in strategy research. Although the term 'strategy' itself has also been interchangeably used with other similar terms such as tactics, skills, or techniques, the critical point is the use of the term 'LLSs'. As Stern (1983) mentioned, the term LLSs has not necessarily been used in the same way by all researchers. The confusion over the term relates primarily to the two following points: (1) whether we should employ the term 'learner strategies' or 'language learning strategies'; and (2) whether we should include communication strategies or not.

Although there seem to be two separate problems in the definition of LLSs, the two points are interconnected. LLSs are usually defined as specific actions taken by the learner to facilitate the obtaining, storage, and retrieval of information (Oxford 1990; Rubin 1987), and LLSs have been recognized as distinct from communication strategies (CSs) in that "the primary purpose for using a learning strategy is not to communicate but to learn" (Tarone 1980: 420). However, the distinction is not so clear according to Dörnyei (1995), who argues that LLSs and CSs can and do overlap.[1] For example, paraphrasing and circumlocution, which are usually categorized as CSs, can also facilitate learning. Learners can strengthen their vocabulary network and may be able to recall necessary words easily by employing these strategies. CSs do not work only in avoiding conversation breakdown, but also act as LLSs because learners can create more opportunities for input and output through continuous communication, which promotes learning. Especially in an EFL learning context, where the necessity for use and the actual input/output opportunities are limited to the classroom, communication strategies play an important role as in avoiding communication breakdowns. In this sense, communication strategies can be recognized as LLSs (Oxford 1990). In fact, in recent years, more researchers use the term 'learner strategies' instead of 'language learning strategies' (Cohen 1998; Dörnyei 1995; McDonough 1999a; Skehan 1991; Wenden 1991) because of the interconnection between LLSs and CSs. In this study, I will use the term 'learner strategies' (henceforth, LSs) to mean 'learning strategies' in a broader sense, which includes communication strategies. These relationships are illustrated in Figure 4.

---

1   Although Tarone (1980) maintained the importance of keeping CSs and LLSs distinct, she also questioned whether it is feasible.

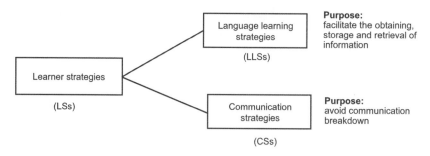

Figure 4. The relationship among LSs, LLSs, and CSs.

2.3.2. Relevant work on learner strategies

2.3.2.1. The Good Language Learner study

Let us now turn to the research literature on learner strategies. Over the past two decades, a considerable number of studies have been conducted on learner strategies. The pioneering works in this area related to L2 learning are Stern (1975), Rubin (1975), and Naiman, Fröhlich, Stern and Todesco (1978/1996). In particular, Naiman *et al.*'s study on good language learners (GLL) is important in that it prompted the further study of individual differences and learner strategies. Their work was extensive and useful, examining GLL research through correlational studies to observe the influence of various learner factors such as gender, learning style, personality, and attitude to L2 learning. Just as Krashen (1982, 1985) triggered further development and elaboration of SLA theory with his ambitious monitor model, Naiman *et al.* opened the 'Pandora's box' of LSs: fundamental issues of LSs were identified and addressed in their study, laying the groundwork for further discussion and debate.

The theoretical assumption of Naiman *et al.* is simple, but significant. The research team assumed that language teaching could be greatly improved by better understanding L2 learners themselves and the L2 learning process itself (Naiman *et al.* 1996: 1). They hypothesized that LSs hold the key to the question of why some learners are successful and others fail. By employing semi-structured interviews, Naiman *et al.* identified the following five effective strategies: good language learners will have an active approach to the task, understand that language is a system, realize language is a means of communication and interaction, manage affective demands successfully, and monitor their L2 performance (1996: 30-33).

The research by Naiman *et al.* can be considered groundbreaking in that they identified the salient strategies of successful language learners, but their study also has its limitations. For example, Skehan (1989) criticizes the research because most of the participants were graduate students or university instructors. In other words, the participants were highly successful and gifted learners – some spoke five languages. Skehan's criticism of the selection of participants points to the possibility that GLL's strategies are used only by highly educated people. Further, Skehan points out that it is not clear whether less successful learners would be able to adopt these strategies, as a systematic comparison of strategy use by successful and less successful learners was not made.

Although Naiman *et al.* limit the universality of their findings due to their research methods, their theoretical assumption has influenced LS researchers and language teachers alike. This assumption can be summarized as follows: "if one could identify the strategies adopted by good language learners and then teach poor language learners to use such strategies, these less effective learners would become more able to handle language learning demands" (Skehan 1998: 264). For SLA researchers, investigating learner factors such as LSs holds the promise of contributing to a better understanding of how languages are learned. For teachers, it has become common to ask why learners in similar learning environments differ in their levels of language proficiency. Similarly, the strategies of GLL might be beneficial to less able learners where the lack of success may be attributed to their poor use of LSs. That is, learners simply may not know how to learn a language.

One of the strengths of LS research is the close relationship between research and practice. As Stern (1983) states, many practitioners are frustrated when the results of SLA research seem remote from the realities of the classroom. This typically results in their treating research as trivial (1983: 53). However, the findings of LS research are closely linked to the realities of language teaching. The theoretical assumptions of LS research symbolized by Naiman *et al.*'s study can be applied to classroom teaching. Thus, the findings of LS research are of benefit to both researchers and practitioners.

2.3.2.2. O'Malley and Chamot's contribution

In the 1980s, O'Malley and Chamot, and their research group conducted a series of studies investigating the nature of LSs (Chamot 1987; O'Malley/Chamot/Stewner-Manzanares/Küpper/Russo 1985a; O'Malley/Chamot/Stewner-Manzanares/Russo/Küpper 1985b). Their contribution was distinctive in the field of strategy research because of its comprehensive approach in the following aspects: (1) the proposal of a classification scheme of strategies; (2) the attempt to teach strategies to students – strategy training; and (3) the attempt to establish a theoretical foundation of strategies.

In their 1985a study, O'Malley et al. identified the range and frequency of strategies used by ESL (English as a second language) high school students in the U.S (N = 70). By conducting retrospective interviews, the researchers revealed 26 types of LLSs (638 tokens) (1985a: 32). Although the list of frequently employed LLSs reported in this series of studies is important, O'Malley and Chamot's most crucial contribution (1990) was their classification of strategies. Prior to this, Rubin (1981) had identified eight strategies and had developed a dichotomous classification scheme – i.e., direct and indirect strategy groups. Based on theories of cognitive psychology, Rubin's classification, and the learner strategies collected from their data, O'Malley and Chamot (1990) developed a tripartite classification scheme – metacognitive, cognitive, and socio-affective – that has been used by many researchers since (e.g., Robbins 1996) and been widely acknowledged as an equally effective classification scheme as Oxford's (Brown 2000; Larsen-Freeman/Long 1991; Mitchell/Myles 1998; Skehan 1989). Metacognitive strategies are "beyond-the-cognitive strategies used to provide executive control over the learning process" (Oxford/Crookall 1989: 404), which are mainly used for arranging, planning, monitoring, and evaluating one's learning.

Metacognitive strategies are especially important in that they enable L2 learners to direct their learning and review their progress (O'Malley/Chamot 1990: 99). Cognitive strategies can be described as

29

"the steps or operations used in learning or problem-solving that require direct analysis, transformation, or synthesis of learning materials" (Rubin 1987: 23), including key word memory, translation, and note-taking strategies. Socio-affective strategies represent "a broad grouping that involves either interaction with another person or ideational control over affect" (O'Malley/Chamot 1990: 45), which encompass such LLSs as co-operating with others, or questioning for clarification.

O'Malley and Chamot (1990) used Anderson's Adaptive Control of Thought (ACT) model (Anderson 1983, 1995) as a theoretical basis for their study. In the ACT model, skill acquisition is explained in three stages: (1) the cognitive stage, in which the procedure is learned in a declarative form and the use of the knowledge is sluggish; (2) the associative stage, where errors in initial understanding are altered and declarative knowledge shifts to procedural knowledge; and (3) the autonomous stage, in which the procedure becomes rapid and automatic (Anderson 1995: 273-275). Briefly stated, the ACT model views skill acquisition as a movement from declarative to procedural knowledge, which rehearsal or practice makes possible. The ACT model explains cognitive skills such as calculation in arithmetic or other general skills such as driving a car. However, not all research demonstrates that, in L2 learning, knowledge shifts from declarative to procedural knowledge, but rather on certain occasions, a movement from the procedural to the declarative occurs (see White/Ranta 2000). In L2 learning, then, the ACT model has less supporting evidence. In learner strategy research, the lack of theoretical foundations constitutes a weakness (Macaro 2006). McDonough (1999b: 58) states: "we have no general theory of strategy use in which they [strategies] can be articulated and their relative importance assessed." However, the ACT model seems to provide a reasonable theoretical basis for L2 learning in an English as a foreign language (EFL) context such as Japan. In many Japanese classrooms, the grammar translation and audio-lingual methods are still used, in which learners first learn the rules of grammar – represented by the cognitive stage – and then try to become fluent in speaking through repeated practice – as observed in both the associative and autonomous stages.

2.3.2.3. Oxford's contribution

Rebecca Oxford has made a significant contribution to and has had a profound influence on strategy research. She proposed a comprehensive six-scheme strategy classification system (Oxford 1986, 1990) and has developed the strategy questionnaire SILL (Strategy Inventory for Language Learning) that is presently widely employed throughout the world (Oxford 1996; Oxford/Burry-Stock 1995). Oxford's (1990) classification system consisting of six components, namely memory, cognitive, compensation, metacognitive, affective, and social strategies, differs from the O'Malley and Chamot scheme due to the inclusion of memory and compensation strategies. As implied in the previous discussion, Oxford's (1990) classification is reasonable when we think about the overlapping character of learning strategies and communication strategies. The validity of the SILL will be discussed in the next chapter.

Using the classification scheme and the SILL, Oxford has conducted a number of studies on LSs. Oxford and Nyikos (1989), for example, examined the strategy use of 1200 university students to see what learner variables affect their choice of strategies. As a result, they found that language proficiency (self-rated), career orientation reflected in university majors, learners' motivation, and sex differences influenced the choice of strategies. In regard to sex differences, Oxford, Nyikos, and Ehrman (1988) also conducted a meta-analysis of four previous studies and uncovered that "frequency and variety of strategy use was significantly greater for women" (1988: 326). With 375 participants at the University of Puerto Rico, Green and Oxford (1995) found that learners of various course levels (prebasic, basic, and intermediate) used different strategies, and that men and women often used different strategies.

If Naiman *et al.* opened the 'Pandora's box' of LSs, Oxford convinced second/foreign language teachers and researchers of the importance of LSs with a user-friendly questionnaire, the SILL. Through the research studies she has conducted, she demonstrated the scope and importance of LSs, which will be summarized in the next section.

2.3.3. Summary and evaluation of research on learner strategies: two paradigms

Reviewing the studies on LSs, there appears to be two research paradigms: (1) a paradigm in which the LSs of good learners became the focus (Paradigm-I); and (2) a paradigm in which the matching of LSs to learners' characteristics was the focus (Paradigm-II).[2] In Paradigm-I, it was theorized that sets of effective LSs that would work universally could be discovered. Studies by Rubin (1975), Stern (1975), and Naiman *et al.* (1978/1996) are typical cases of Paradigm-I, as the research titles themselves reveal. Here the crucial aspect is *'the'* good language learner, not *'a'* good language learner.

Naiman *et al.* (1978/1996)	Rubin (1975, 1981)
1. Active task approach	Clarification/verification Memorization
2. Language is a system	Guessing, inductive inferencing Deductive reasoning
3. Monitoring of performance	Monitoring
4. Language is a means of communication and interaction	
5. Management of affective demands	

Table 2. Comparison of findings from earlier strategy research about Paradigm-I (adapted from Skehan 1989: 81).

Although in this paradigm, the connection with or the influence of other factors such as gender, nationality, or the major field of study at university was considered, the assumption was that good language learners employ distinct and effective LSs that less effective learners do not use but can learn. As Skehan (1989) made known in his comparison between early studies of LSs, the findings of the first paradigm provided a general understanding of LSs and had implications for effective teaching and learning as demonstrated in Table 2. The underlying premise of this paradigm was useful, but as the research to identify the impact of LSs increased, the results were found to be more complex (e.g., Vann/Abraham 1990).

---

2   I coined the terms strategy Paradigm-I and -II.

Although the quest for 'the' good LSs has continued until the present (Bruen 2001, Griffiths 2003, Porte 1988, Takeuchi 2003a, Wharton 2000), this research showed that a new paradigm was needed. In the mid 1990s, MacIntyre and Noels (1994) postulated that LSs should not be considered apart from other learner characteristics and environments. The current assumption is that everyone has the potential to be a good language learner if he/she learns to use the appropriate strategies to tap their own strengths or to compensate for their own weaknesses (MacIntyre/Noels 1994). In fact, factors such as age, motivation, personality, and gender are reported to affect the choice of LSs (Ehrman/Oxford 1990, Oxford/Nyikos 1989, Reiss 1985). In the first paradigm, the main focus is on the effects of LSs in relation to English proficiency, not on the relationship of LSs with other learner characteristics, because LSs are assumed to be the causal factor. In the second paradigm, however, the role of LSs is considered to be influenced by various learners' characteristics as well as influencing some of them. In short, various sets of LSs that depend on learners' characteristics can exist simultaneously to improve English proficiency; that is, not the particular set of LSs of 'good language learners,' but rather an individualized set of LSs. Such an idea is parallel to the paradigm shift in teaching methods toward student-centered education; although Communicative Language Teaching is dominant in current English education in the 21st century, it cannot be a panacea for all learners. Indeed, the grammar translation method is not totally ignored – it might be the preferred and most effective way of instruction for some learners. The important thing here is that we should not conclude that there exists an absolute set of LSs that will work for every learner. Instead, there should be various routes to learning to attain high English proficiency. In this sense, we need to return to Skehan's learning model (see Figure 1) where LSs were recognized as catalytic agents to mediate learner factors and English proficiency.

In both paradigms, LSs are significant in that "we can gain insights into the cognitive, social and affective processes involved in language learning" (Chamot 2001: 25). While teachers believe that they know learners well, in fact, research shows that they do not know as much as they think they do about their students. O'Malley et al. (1985a), for example, interviewed high school students and their teachers about which strategies students were employing. Students reported using an average of 33.6 strategies in the classroom, but teachers identified only 25.4 strategies that they thought students were using. Such a discrepancy points to the fact that teachers are not fully aware of their learners' ways of learning (35). Good language teachers have an intuitive understanding of language learning (Naiman *et al.* 1978/1996); yet they may lack a systematic understanding of the differences among learners. By incorporating learner strategies into teaching strategies, teachers can tailor their way of teaching to the strategies language learners are using, which may result in more effective teaching.

Clearly, learner strategy research can assist in opening avenues to an enhanced systematic understanding of learners. Furthermore, teachers can incorporate these crucial learner strategies into their approach and methodologies. Indeed, this is an important part of the rationale for focusing on LSs in the present study.

2.3.4. The issue of strategy training

Connected to the two research paradigms of LSs, the issue of strategy training, or strategy-based instruction (SBI: Cohen 1998) is a contro-versial area (Rees-Miller 1993). Originally, the issue stemmed from Paradigm I and the question of whether it is possible to teach strategies of good language learners to less successful learners. Skepticism first originated from a theoretical point of view. Dörnyei (1995) summa-rized the justification for and against providing strategy training: 1) strategies *need not* be taught because learners are already familiar with strategies from their first language use; 2) strategies *cannot be* taught because strategies are the surface realization of underlying psycholo-gical processes, and strategies vary in their teachability (i.e., some strategies are easy to teach but some are difficult). Dörnyei (2005) further argues that the impact of teaching learning strategies is hard to assess because the relationship between learning strategies and English proficiency is not linear. In contrast, training of communication strate-gies is possible because they are related to speech production.

34

On the other hand, to date there is an accumulation of empirical studies about teaching strategies. Dörnyei (1995), for example, investigated the effect of teaching three communication strategies – fillers, topic avoidance, and circumlocutions – to 109 secondary school Hungarian students learning English as a foreign language through a 6-week training program, and found an increase in the use of circumlocutions and fillers, and significant improvement in learners' speech rate.

Cohen, Weaver, and Li (1996) reported the effect of SBI on 55 university students learning French or Norwegian. They found an increase in the strategies taught such as monitoring strategies to pay attention to the pronunciation of words or to analyze a story, and a significant relationship between strategy use and performance on speaking tasks.

Swain (2000) reported on Holunga's (1994) strategy training research about the effects of metacognitive strategy training and verbalization on the accurate usage of verb forms. Holunga compared three groups of students: the MV group, which received training in metacognitive strategies such as predicting, planning, monitoring, or evaluating and were also instructed to verbalize those strategies; the M group, which received training in the metacognitive strategies but were not given instructions to verbalize; and the C group, which were not given either. All the participants were advanced second language learners of English, who received 15 hours of ESL instruction in the course of study. Holunga found that the MV group were able to use verbs more accurately than the other two groups. MV group students accurately produced the appropriate verb form (e.g., *needs*, instead of *need*) and through collaborative dialogue, they even talked about how they could improve their accuracy in using verbs. This study indicates that the combination of strategy training and verbalization of the strategies enables students to make much more effective use of the strategies they have learned.

In her study, Paulauskas (1994) provided training in listening comprehension strategies to two groups of high beginner/low intermediate ESL students. The strategies included 'predicting text content', 'summarizing main information', 'questioning for comprehension of main ideas' and 'clarifying comprehension difficulties.' The researcher found that the two groups performed significantly better on listening tests than the control group, who received the same instructional materials, but no strategy training.

Yang (2003) also investigated the effectiveness of SBI by encouraging 45 Taiwanese college students to use metacognitive strategies by keeping portfolios to self-reflect on their learning plans and to monitor their progress in English. He found an increase in listening proficiency and in students' awareness of strategy use.

Dadour and Robbins (1996) reported the effectiveness of a 15-week strategy instruction on 122 Egyptian university students taking a teacher preparation program. Training in the use of speaking strategies for a specific linguistic/conversational speaking skill was provided; the researchers reported positive effects of strategy training on fluency, vocabulary usage, and grammar.

Huang (2004) also reported the effects of strategy training on speaking. She provided a strategy-use awareness session over 10 weeks with advanced adult ESL learners, and found a statistically significant positive effect on oral production.

Kern (1989) explored the effect of explicit instruction of second language (French) reading comprehension strategies such as word analysis strategies using cognates, prefixes or suffixes, and sentence and discourse analysis strategies with 53 college students in California. He evaluated his strategy training as successful: "reading strategy training had a strong positive effect on L2 readers' comprehension gain scores" (143).

Besides these studies, practical guide books of teaching and learning strategies for teachers and learners have been published. Ellis and Sinclair (1989) presented strategies to improve vocabulary, grammar, listening, speaking, reading, and writing in their classic book. Chamot and O'Malley (1994) developed a systematic approach, the Cognitive Academic Language Learning Approach (CALLA), which incorporates strategy training into communicative language teaching, and Chamot, Barnhardt, El-Dinary, and Robbins (1999) made CALLA easily applicable for language teachers and learners by showing many classroom activities so that they can understand how to use strategies by engaging in those activities.

Empirical data thus seem to show that strategy training can have a positive effect on learners' English proficiency and their use of strategies, but strategy training has not always contributed to learner success.

In their attempt to teach effective strategies, for example, O'Malley *et al.* (1985b) sought to determine if there was a significant effect of strategy training on vocabulary learning, listening comprehension and speaking. The participants of this study were 75 high school students, learning English as a second language in the U.S. They were separated into three groups: a metacognitive group, where a combination of metacognitive, cognitive, and socio-affective strategies were taught; a cognitive group, in which instruction on both cognitive and socio-affective strategies was given; and a control group, where the participants were asked to work on language learning tasks in their usual way, without any special strategy instruction. Specifically, in the metacognitive group, three strategies – self-evaluation (for vocabulary), selective attention (for listening), and functional planning (for speaking) – were taught. With respect to cognitive strategies, students were trained in imagery and grouping (for vocabulary), and note-taking (for listening), though no strategies were presented for speaking. As to the socio-affective strategies, cooperation was taught for listening and speaking; no strategies were presented for vocabulary learning. After the eight-day strategy instruction, the effects on vocabulary, listening, and speaking proficiency were assessed. Statistically significant effects were observed only in speaking and one section of the listening tests. The metacognitive group scored highest and the cognitive group scored higher than the control group. O'Malley *et al.*'s research indicated that the more LSs the learners have, the higher the level of achievement they can reach. However, we must be prudent about deciding that strategy training works because only a small set of strategies was arbitrarily selected for instruction (Skehan 1989: 90).

Wenden (1987a) reported a project to increase the metacognitive awareness of 23 advanced learners by providing them with a chance to read materials adapted from materials about language learning and to discuss language learning in class. The questionnaire after the training session was less positive because only seven had changed their approach and five had learned something new about language learning.

More than half of the participants answered that training was not useful. She concluded that "learner training was not considered relevant in its own right" (164).

Thus, we must not jump to conclusions about the usefulness of strategy training because we still do not know which strategies should be taught in the first place or whether the trained strategies consistently contributed to increasing English proficiency. As Bialystok (1985) predicted, the effects of teaching strategies depend on learner characteristics, his/her purpose in learning the language, and the conditions or context in which SBI programs are carried out.

2.4. Environmental factors and English proficiency: EFL learning conditions in Japan

2.4.1. ESL and EFL

The distinction between ESL (English as a second language) and EFL (English as a foreign language) is widely acknowledged by SLA researchers, but sometimes its critical role in L2 learning has been discounted, as seen in the following quotation: "This [ESL-EFL] difference in setting is of very great practical importance to teachers. [...] While not denying the importance of the distinction, I will use the terms interchangeably" (Bley-Vroman 1989: 43). However, it is perhaps arguable, as I will go on to propose, that the difference between ESL and EFL is crucial in both a theoretical and a practical sense, and in particular for learner autonomy, and for the quality and quantity of input and output. Therefore, these terms cannot be used interchangeably.

The characteristics of English learning in an EFL context are succinctly summarized in the following three points: (1) there are few opportunities for using the target language outside the classroom; (2) teachers are often non-native speakers (NNSs) of the target language; and (3) there is little time for foreign language instruction (Krashen 1997: 39). The Japanese educational system offers limited exposure to

English as a result of the small amount of time allocated to English lessons. For example, Japanese public junior high school students in 2000 received three to four hours a week (in 50-minute blocks) of English lessons at school. The total amount of time that these students will learn English at school in a year is estimated to be 144 hours at most; yet sometimes classes are cut due to special programs or national holidays, so that the total amount of instruction amounts to 432 hours in three years, which is equivalent to a scant 27 days (based on MEXT 1989). On the other hand, although it is difficult to generalize because there are various kinds of ESL programs in North America, according to Takashima (1990: 111), ESL students attending an ESL program in a North American school may be exposed to 1,268 hours of English instruction in a year, and 3,804 hours in three years, which results in 237.6 days. This is 8.8 times greater than the total of English input in a Japanese public junior high school. It should be noted that the estimate of the input in the Japanese junior high school is based on the assumption that English lessons in Japan are provided through the target language, whereas in fact they are sometimes offered through the native language (JACET[3] Education Research Group 2001). Thus, exposure to English is more limited than this estimate presumes because in most cases NNSs are responsible for the English classes.

Many researchers agree on the importance of comprehensible input (Doughty/Williams 1998, Long 1996) for developing second language abilities, and it is clear that exposure to the target language is the basis for comprehensible input. In this regard, if learners want to develop their proficiency in English in an EFL context, they will inevitably need to allot more time for English learning or exposure to English outside the classroom. This points to the fact that self-directed learning and effective use of strategies for autonomous learning are indispensable in an EFL context. It can be concluded, from what has been argued above, that paying attention to the learning context is important.

---

3 JACET stands for Japan Association of College English Teachers.

2.4.2. Factors specific to Japan

Japanese junior and senior high school classrooms traditionally have not provided optimal conditions for language teaching and learning. Students learn English in large classes: the government specifies that the maximum number is 40 students per class.[4] Such learning conditions are inadequate compared to other economically developed countries such as the U.S., Canada, or Germany, where a normal class size is approximately 25 students per class (e.g., U.S. Department of Education 2000). Under such circumstances, Japanese students have tended not to fully participate in classes, often refraining entirely from speaking. They rarely engage in spontaneous interactions with their teacher or their fellow classmates; otherwise, teachers would not be able to maintain the control over classes that they have. It would appear that students have been trained to act as passive learners, remaining silent even when questions emerge in their minds; they have been encouraged to respond and inquire only when they are called upon.

However, today in Japan, some significant changes are occurring in English classes. The recent *Course of Study* (MEXT 1989, 1998) encourages teachers to adopt a communicative approach as a teaching method to foster the communicative competence of students. MEXT, which controls the curricula and textbooks for English classes, is now enthusiastically promoting English oral proficiency. Although students' behavior in other classes remains passive, recently students have been required to behave actively in their English classes. Teachers are encouraging students to speak up and participate actively in English by working in pairs, groups or on a whole class basis. Teachers are trying to involve students in communicative activities such as 'information gap', and other communicative games. This is a somewhat amusing change because students have suddenly been asked to act as active learners only in their English classes, learning conditions remaining unchanged in other classes. According to this, I would expect that some

---

4   In fact, according to MEXT (2005), the average number of students per class has been decreasing because of a declining birthrate in Japan: it was 32.4 in 2000, and was 30.7 in 2005.

learners, especially introverted learners, would feel anxious about English classes, and feel further isolated from the learning process.

2.4.3. Rationale for use of listening as an evaluative tool

Listening has an important meaning for Japanese learners of English. The choice of the listening ability as an evaluative tool was thus made in view of the characteristics of recent English learning conditions in Japan, as well as of learners' strong motivation to improve their listening proficiency. In this section, the rationale behind using this tool in this study, in terms of: a) new trends in junior or senior high schools, b) popularity of the TOEIC (Test of English for International Communication; see Section 3.2.2.5), and c) the relationship of listening to E/I and LSs, will be stated.

Although the four skills of speaking, reading, writing, and listening are important, as stated in the latest *Course of Study* (MEXT 1998, 1999), the oral/aural skills of listening and speaking are now being stressed in Japan. MEXT states that the overall objectives of teaching English in Japanese junior high schools is "to develop students' basic practical communication abilities such as listening and speaking" in addition to "deepening the understanding of language and culture, and fostering a positive attitude toward communication through foreign languages" (MEXT 1998: 88). In fact, MEXT has been trying to shift the focus of English teaching in Japan from grammar to communication since the 1990s. Towards that eventuality, in high schools, MEXT specified in their important revised policy document (1989) that every school needed to teach one oral skills course (*Oral A, B or C*) focusing on listening and speaking skills. Indeed the latest revision increased the number of courses, emphasizing oral skills such as *English I* as well as *Oral I* or *II* (MEXT 1998, 1999).

In the classroom, however, many teachers have ignored the intentions of MEXT, and have continued to use the traditional grammar translation method (Yoshida 2003), and spend little time on teaching listening or speaking.[5] This is best illustrated by the fact that when

---

5   As to this issue, Yoshida (2003: 291) argues that "the problem with teaching

Takanashi (1999) observed an *Oral A* course, grammar teaching for preparation for university entrance exams was provided instead of listening or speaking, and the course was sometimes sarcastically called the *Oral Grammar* course by students (also noted by Yoshida 2003). Reflecting on such problematic situations, MEXT decided to introduce a listening test as part of the standard college entrance exam starting in 2006 to encourage more communicative language teaching in the classroom, because the traditional entrance exam, which focused on reading comprehension, was assumed to be one of the culprits causing the inadequacies of Japanese English language teaching and learning.

Interestingly and conversely, after entering the university, learners tend to devote much more time to listening than to other skills. This is because they are concerned with obtaining good test scores in the TOEIC or the TOEFL (Test of English as a Foreign Language), both of which include a listening section but not a speaking section.[6] Learners are accustomed to reading comprehension or grammar tests, so they believe they do not need additional preparation for those sections of the test. Especially among the college student population in Japan, the number of test-takers of the TOEIC has been increasing for the last several years, partly because higher scores on the TOEIC are known to be beneficial for finding employment after graduation. Japanese universities encourage students to take the TOEIC test and sometimes make the test compulsory or subsidize the cost. Although this does not mean that the TOEIC is the best measurement of English proficiency, the TOEIC is the proficiency test most familiar to Japanese college students.

As a third reason for using the listening ability in this study, it is my hypothesis that listening will be influenced by E/I. The exposure to English in Japan is often restricted to English classes, which constitutes a considerable difference from learning in ESL contexts. If learners intend to develop their listening proficiency in an EFL context,

---

English in Japan, then, is how the ideals envisioned in the government language education policy (LEP) can be implemented in actual teaching practice".

6   The new TOEFL test (iBT: Internet-based Test) that includes a speaking section started in July 2006, and the new TOEIC test with speaking was launched in 2007 in Japan. These changes had an influence on students' goals toward learning English.

they inevitably need to allot more time for English learning or exposure to English outside the classroom. Thus, making effective use of LSs is indispensable in an EFL context. I did a preliminary study to compare the use of LSs by Es and Is, and found that extroverts used significantly more strategies to increase their exposure to English (Wakamoto 2000). For example, extroverts spent more time watching English language TV shows, going to movies in English, or practicing English with other students (77). Such strategies, especially increased exposure to English, should help students improve their listening proficiency. Considering the characteristics of learning settings in Japan where input or output opportunities are limited to the classroom, this kind of strategy use will likely influence listening proficiency. Of course, other factors such as knowledge of grammar or vocabulary will also affect listening comprehension. However, from the perspective of strategies that learners employ, we might hypothesize that extroverts are more adept at improving listening than are introverts. This hypothesis constitutes part of the rationale to focus on the listening proficiency of learners in Japan.

As to listening strategies themselves, those of metacognitive strategies such as comprehension monitoring or problem identification have been shown to be used by skilled listeners (Vandergrift 1996, 1997, 1998), and as I have stated earlier, teaching of metacognitive strategies to Taiwanese college students was found to contribute to developing college students' listening proficiency (Yang 2003). However, my study focuses on how learners use strategies to increase the amount and quality of input in an EFL context. Listening proficiency is used to evaluate how well students have used input enhancing strategies. Although this study will concentrate on the listening skill rather than others, the main focus is to observe the impact of E/I on how learners study English differently, and eventually to investigate how such differences influence their English ability.

2.5. Research questions

The goal of this study is two-fold: (1) to describe the general use of LSs of Japanese learners of English, and to examine whether extroverts or introverts show differentiated use of LS; and (2) to identify the impact of extroversion/introversion on language learning in terms of learner strategies and English proficiency. Thus the research questions are as follows:

1. What are the characteristic LSs of Japanese college students in the EFL context?
2. What are the characteristic LSs of extroverts and introverts in the Japanese college context?
3. Do extroversion and introversion have an impact on proficiency in English as a foreign language, in particular on college learners' listening proficiency?

2.6. Significance of the study

As Dewaele and Furnham (1999) state, only a limited number of research studies have dealt with extroversion/introversion to date. However, as mentioned earlier, there are good theoretical and empirical reasons to investigate the impact of E/I on language learning. Identifying the relationship between E/I, learner strategies and English proficiency can make a unique contribution to the field: in other words, it can identify how extroverts and introverts can make better use of LSs. Extroverts (Es) and introverts (Is) can become aware of their strengths and weaknesses, and can adopt appropriate learner strategies that will enhance their strengths and compensate for their weaknesses. This is especially important for an EFL learning context, where naturalistic English learning cannot be expected to occur, and learners need to acquire and use appropriate strategies to improve their English proficiency.

44

3. Methods

3.1. Introduction

This chapter describes the methodologies applied in this study, which consist of three phases: (1) Phase I, a quantitative data analysis of a LS questionnaire, listening proficiency test, and a measure of E/I of participants; (2) Phase II, a qualitative data analysis based on classroom observations and stimulated recall interviews with two participants; and (3) Phase III, a qualitative data analysis based on the completion of a task in an individual learning context (by two participants). The overall research design is illustrated in Figure 5.

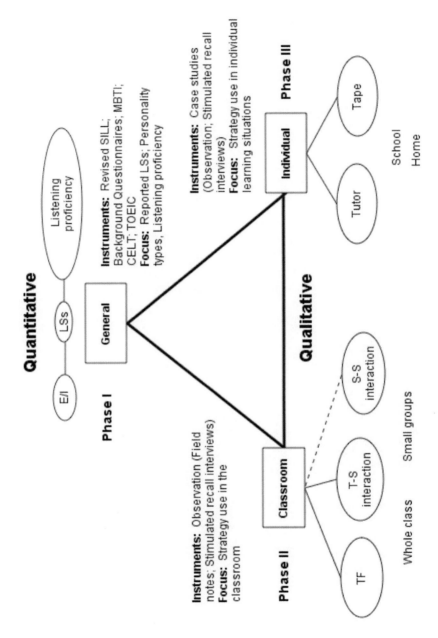

Figure 5. Overall design of this study: Phase I, II, and III.

To reiterate the main purpose of this study, it is to examine the impact of E/I on listening proficiency and on LSs. To attain this objective, in Phase I (top point of the triangle in Figure 5), quantitative data were relied upon, with particular stress placed on the LSs reported in the questionnaires. Then the impact of extroversion and introversion (personality types) on LSs and listening proficiency was measured by standardized listening proficiency tests. To triangulate the results of Phase I, students' strategy use in the classroom (left edge of the triangle in Figure 5) and in individual learning situations (right edge of the triangle in Figure 5) were the main focus. In the classroom, teacher-fronted situations (henceforth, TF) and teacher-student interactions (T-S) in small groups were closely examined. Student-student interactions (S-S) in small groups were not emphasized for the following reason: through the classroom observations and interviews with eight students, it was found that learners hesitated to communicate in English with each other. When they had problems in maintaining communication with other learners, they switched to Japanese and asked about or confirmed the information in their native language. In other words, in group activities students were using strategies in Japanese, not in English. Because my main emphasis was on strategy use in English, I therefore decided to focus on teacher-student interactions rather than student-student interactions. This did not completely eliminate small group data because some students used LSs with the teacher as representatives of their small groups.

For classroom observations, I used field notes and stimulated recall interviews. In the individual learning situations, I observed the use of strategies in interacting either with a tutor or with a tape recorder.

3.2. Phase I

3.2.1. Context and participants

The participants in this study were 148 second-year college students who were learning English in Japan. To avoid the influence of gender interaction (between men and women) and age effects, the participants were all female, and their ages ranged from 19 to 21. Participants were recruited from a women's college, one of the most prestigious liberal arts colleges in Japan with a long history. The college has about 5,000 students majoring in various fields: Music, Japanese Language and Literature, Social Studies, Clinical Pharmacy, Food Studies and Nutrition, and English, and although this college emphasizes internationalism as well as Christianity and liberal arts, the number of foreign students in all departments is small. Furthermore, the interest of students in departments other than English to learn the English language is low in general. For these reasons, all the participants recruited were English majors. However, although all the participants were English major students, their language levels varied greatly.

3.2.2. Instruments

3.2.2.1. Personality questionnaire

In order to judge and measure which students were extroverts, and which were introverts, the Japanese version of the Myers-Briggs Type Indicator (MBTI-Form G) was employed. The MBTI is a self-report type questionnaire based on Jung's (1987) psychology, which was first created by Isabel Myers and Katharine Briggs in 1942, and since then has been continuously refined by a group of international psychologists (e.g., Quenk/Hammer/Majors 2001). The MBTI is one of the best-known questionnaires presently being used in second language acquisition research (Ehrman 1996, Brown 2000), along with the EPI (Eysenck Personality Inventory: Eysenck/Eysenck 1968, 1975) and with the

Sixteen Personality Factor Questionnaire developed by Cattell (16PF: Cattell 1989), to measure personality characteristics.

While the EPI offers information on the extroversion/introversion of people as well as neuroticism/stability by continuous numerical scales, the MBTI offers information on the human character by sorting people into 16 types through combinations of the following four bi-polar subscales: extroversion-introversion, perceiving-judging, sensing-intuition, and thinking-feeling (Myers 2000). The MBTI has also been widely used for counseling, self-understanding, understanding others, and career development in both schools and companies. However, in this study, it was only necessary to exploit the information that related to extroversion/introversion, so all other information was disregarded.

The difference between the MBTI and other instruments such as the EPI is that while the MBTI yields dichotomous information, i.e., extroversion or introversion, with preference scores (PSs), other instruments present the information by interval scales that will decide the degree of respondents' E/I. In the case of the MBTI, PSs indicate how clearly respondents' E/I appear. Table 3 presents four categorizations of extroversion and introversion.

Preference score (PS)	Indication of preference (IP)	Interpretation
1-9	Slight preference	A change of one or two question items could change to the opposite pole of the dichotomy.
10-19	Moderate preference	Respondents make habitual use of one or more aspects of the opposite pole of the dichotomy.
20-49	Clear preference	There is a reasonable probability that the respondents hold and act on the preference.
50-	Very clear preference	Respondents hold most of the characteristics that accompany preferences.

Table 3. Categorization of E/I by preference scores (adapted from adapted from Myers/ McCaulley/Quenk/Hammer 1998 and Sonoda 2000).

Table 3 indicates that in respondents with 'moderate' or 'slight' preferences their E/I does not manifest itself clearly. In an analysis of the impact of E/I on LSs or listening proficiency, taking into account respondents with moderate or slight preferences would make it difficult to clearly uncover the impact of E/I on foreign language learning.

Although the MBTI generates dichotomous information, converting it into continuous numbers is feasible based on the following validated formula (Sonoda 2000): continuous values for extroversion = 100 - IP (Indication of Preference in Table 3) scores; and continuous values for introversion = 100 + IP. Based on this formula, high validity and reliability of the MBTI was established (Sonoda 2000). With the NEO (Neuroticism Extroversion Openness) Personality Inventory (NEO-PI: Costa/McCrae 1992), for example, the MBTI showed significantly high correlations (Pearson product-moment correlation coefficient: $r = .74$ for male and $r = .69$ for female; n = 468) (Myers/McCaulley/Quenk/Hammer 1998).[7] The reliability of the Japanese version (Form G) has also been tested in several ways (Sonoda 2000). The internal consistency (Spearman-Brown) of the E/I subscale was .91 (n = 114). The test-retest correlation coefficient was acceptably high ($r = .876$; n = 45), and the Pearson correlation coefficient between the English version of the MBTI (Form G) and that of the Japanese version was also high ($r = .856$; n = 19). In order to uncover the E/I of participants, it would have been possible to use alternative instruments like EPI or the NEO-PI. However, the main reasons for adopting the MBTI were its confirmed high validity and reliability, and the fact that it has been translated into Japanese. In personality questionnaires, participants are usually asked to judge whether or not they will adopt a given behavior. In this sense, to provide a questionnaire in the native language of the respondents is important so that participants can understand the meaning of each item fully. Other personality questionnaires have yet to be developed in Japanese versions.

3.2.2.2. Instructor's holistic evaluation of learners' E/I

To triangulate the MBTI results, I included the course instructor's holistic evaluation of learners' E/I. A course instructor of an oral com-

---

7   MBTI has a statistically significant correlation with the 16PF: the 16PF extroversion global factor showed positive correlation with the MBTI as regards the extroversion type ($r = . 68$) and negative correlation with the introversion type ($r = -.61$) by a study administered to 119 students (Russell/Karol 1994).

munication class that was selected for Phase II was asked to evaluate participants' (n = 38; participants of two classes) degree of E/I holistically by the numbers of 1 (highly extroverted) to 7 (highly introverted). To aid the instructor in making a holistic evaluation, characteristics of extroverts and introverts were explained using Table 1, and it was confirmed that the course instructor understood the concepts of E/I. Then, the relationship between the MBTI results and the course instructor's holistic evaluation was tested using the Pearson correlation coefficient. The result of this is reported in Section 4.2.4.2.

3.2.2.3. Strategy questionnaire for reported strategies

A questionnaire, which can be defined as a "self-report data-collection instrument that each research participant fills out as part of a research study" (Johnson/Christensen 2000: 127), is often used to uncover learners' attitudes, beliefs, motivation, and LSs in research on individual learner characteristics (Skehan 1991). Questionnaires are used because observing learner variables entails substantial difficulties: for example, some LSs are invisible and unobservable, and even for visible strategies, it is impractical to track learners outside the classroom to observe their use of LSs. It follows that we need to rely at least in part on questionnaires to elicit information on learners' use of LSs.

Although I recognize the importance of questionnaires in the research on LSs, I have found some aspects of strategy questionnaires problematic. The strategy questionnaire used in this study was based on the SILL, one of the most frequently used and widely accepted LS questionnaires in use throughout the world for investigating LSs (Bedell/Oxford 1996). While reviewing the drawbacks of the SILL, it will be appropriate to describe how and why it was essential to modify it.

Firstly, the lack of contextualization or examples causes discrepancies and difficulties in assessing individual learner characteristics. LoCastro (1994) conducted research to observe the salient LSs of university students in Japan, and one particularly interesting finding from her study came out when she asked the participants to talk about how they felt when answering the SILL. LoCastro concludes that the SILL lacks contextualization and that it is as a consequence difficult to answer some of the items (412). One example given in her paper is that to respond to the item 'I start conversations in English' (the SILL for ESL/EFL Version 7.0, No. 14; Oxford 1990: 295), the learner needs more contextual information. Such potentially ambiguous items should be either deleted or improved by providing examples that illustrate the questions (Johnson 1992). In the process of modifying the SILL for this study, examples were added to clarify potentially ambiguous items.

Secondly, a problem arises in relation to learning contexts. The difference of learning contexts in questionnaire research creates bias and blurs attempts to assess the characteristics of individual learners. In L2 learning, for example, the distinction between ESL and EFL is widely recognized (see Section 2.4.1). The characteristics of L2 learning in an EFL context are best summarized as having few opportunities for using English outside the classroom (Krashen 1997: 39). Naturally, such salient features will influence L2 learning. LoCastro (1994) argued that the ESL-EFL distinction is crucial when it comes to LS, and that the SILL does not pay sufficient attention to the difference in the learning environments, in particular to the EFL learning context. In fact, whereas the SILL has two versions – one for English speakers learning a new language and one for ESL/EFL learners – the second version does not make any distinction between ESL and EFL. The dominance of ESL in the SILL can be attributed to the fact that Oxford field-tested the SILL in the process of developing it with American university and military participants in the U.S (Oxford 1990: 255). Responding to LoCastro, Oxford and Green (1995: 168) argued that the SILL cannot list all possible LSs; and that qualitative methods – case studies, for example – would be more suitable to catalogue the LSs in greater detail. Although listing all LSs is unrealistic, adding characteristic strategies for specific learning contexts is needed. In fact, quite a few studies on LSs have been conducted utilizing a revised SILL that was modified to specific learning conditions (Oxford 1996). In the revised SILL used in this study, several LSs widely used in the EFL learning context in Japan were added after a group of researchers (including Barbara Fujiwara, Kathleen Kitao, and Osamu Takeuchi) carefully considered and discussed the categories in the LS literature. For example, reading aloud has been one of the most frequently used LSs in Japan (Suzuki 1998), and Internet-related LSs also have come to be recognized as significant for EFL learners in general (Warschauer 1996).

Finally, the questionnaire does not necessarily elicit information on the actual use of strategies. The SILL rubric requires language learners to select the response that indicates how true the statement is "in terms of what they actually do when they are learning" (Oxford 1990: 283). However, researchers have reservations about whether the SILL actually taps learners' use of strategies (e.g., LoCastro 1994). In the strict sense, "the *USE* ratings reflect the respondents' impressions of their strategy use" (Schmitt/McCarthy 1997: 236). In this study, to compensate for this weakness and to capture learners' actual use of strategies, three other ratings were employed (henceforth, dimensions) in addition to the use ratings: strategy helpfulness, previous strategy use, and preferences. The helpfulness rating was used in Schmitt (1997), the rating of previous strategy use was used in Kagata (1998), and I added the preference rating.

We cannot expect even carefully modified questionnaires to provide a "rich picture of the complex and interacting social, cultural, linguistic, and cognitive factors" (Johnson 1992: 128). Oxford and Green (1995: 167) themselves also state that the SILL and other such questionnaires just provide "a good general picture of strategy use". We should recognize that questionnaires have different functions from other data collection methods. When we seek rich information on individual learners, other types of verbal reports, as Cohen proposed (1987a, 1987b, 1994), are called for. In this study, observation and stimulated recall interviews were used for that purpose.

I based my questionnaire on LSs on the SILL due to its high reliability and validity (Oxford 1990). While being careful not to change the framework of the SILL, I made the following modifications for Japanese participants: (1) a translation into Japanese; (2) the addition of examples to clarify ambiguous items; (3) the division of items that included more than one strategy; (4) the addition of strategy items specific to Japanese learning contexts; (5) the addition of significant communication strategies; and (6) the deletion of possibly misleading items.

In adapting the SILL, I also referred to two strategy questionnaires developed in Japan: the Language Laboratory Association version of Strategy Inventory (LLASI, 1998), and the Eigo-Jugyoken-kyugakkai version of Strategy Inventory (EJSI, 1998). The LLASI is a translation of the original SILL (ESL/EFL version), which was carefully translated into Japanese through the discussions and consensus of twelve researchers in Japan. The EJSI is also a Japanese translated questionnaire developed by a group of researchers and English teachers in junior or senior high schools within the framework of the SILL (ESL/EFL version). The difference between the LLASI and the EJSI is that the EJSI was designed for Japanese classes – from junior high school through university level – by adding Japan-specific strategy items and examples to clarify ambiguous strategy items. To provide examples of Japan-specific strategy items, I borrowed relevant items from the EJSI. Furthermore, to add important communication strategies, I referred to Dörnyei (1995). By administering the LLASI to Japanese university students, the researchers discovered strategy items that a significantly large number of participants could not answer (Takeuchi/Tanaka/Mishima/Nakanishi/Fukuchi 1998; Takeuchi/Waka-moto 2001). Based on these findings, I removed such items from the original SILL. As to communication strategies, besides the original questionnaire items of the SILL, I referred to Bialystok (1990), Dör-nyei (1995), and Dörnyei/Scott (1995), and added items on avoidance strategies (item 31), use of fillers (item 30) or use of hesitation devices (item 32).

Following the procedures I have described above, I completed a preliminary version of the strategy questionnaire consisting of 89 items (the modified SILL: Appendix A, B). I field-tested the preliminary strategy questionnaire on 102 Japanese students – all female university students, age range from 18 to 20 – in the winter of 2001 (December 6). The purpose of the field test was to uncover problematic items, and to see whether this 89-item version was practical for use. For improvements, I asked participants to write comments or questions about this questionnaire. From the comments participants wrote, I discovered the following two opinions: firstly, that they considered the questionnaire to include an excess of items, secondly that task-dependent items could be misleading. Learners, for example, use a translation strategy – 'translating English sentences into my native language' (the SILL for ESL/EFL Version 7.0, No. 22; Oxford 1990: 295) – differently depending on the task they face: they tend to make full use of this strategy when reading intensively, but are inclined not to rely on it when they read English sentences extensively. The use of some LSs varies depending on the purpose of the task, or changes from year to year, or even day to day (Brown 2000). Although all the LSs are to some extent task dependent, some overtly task dependent items existed in the preliminary questionnaire.

Based on the results of this field test, I revised the preliminary questionnaire. Through the process of removing overtly task dependent questionnaire items, while referring to the SILL, the LLASI, and the EJSI and engaging in discussions with other researchers (including Sharon Lapkin, Barbara Fujiwawa, Kathleen Kitao, and Osamu Takeuchi), I arrived at a questionnaire of 61 items with four dimensions – use, preferences, helpfulness, previous use – for this study (the revised SILL: Appendix B). A statistical validation procedure of this revised version of the questionnaire such as using item analyses was not undertaken.

3.2.2.4. Background questionnaire

In order to obtain the background information of the participants – experiences abroad or opportunities of being exposed to English outside the classroom – a separate questionnaire was designed. The background questionnaire was inspired by the background question-naire created by Oxford (1990). It was carefully composed so that it could collect information on past experiences of studying English in Japan and abroad (see Appendix C).

3.2.2.5. Listening proficiency tests

In order to assess participants' listening proficiency, the listening section of two standardized tests was applied: the TOEIC and the Comprehensive English Language Test (CELT). The TOEIC was ori-ginally created by the Educational Testing Service (ETS) in the 1960s, and is now owned by a subsidiary of ETS (Buck 2001). The TOEIC has been increasingly used in Japanese educational and business contexts. In Japan, the EIKEN (EIgo KENtei in Japanese: Standard Test for English Proficiency by the Society for Testing English

Proficiency) had been the most frequently used standardized English proficiency test for the last three decades, but the number of candidates taking the TOEIC has recently outnumbered those taking the Eiken and other standardized English proficiency tests in Japan. In terms of general English listening ability, it is reasonable to use such a popular English proficiency test because the score can be compared to the norms of the whole test-taking population, in addition to its high reliability and validity. The TOEIC is a machine scorable test consisting of two sections: Listening Comprehension (Part I) and Reading Comprehension (Part II). The possible score range of each section is from 5 to 495.

The CELT is also a standardized test consisting of vocabulary, reading, and listening sections with two forms: Form A and Form B. The minimum and maximum scores for the each section of the CELT are 0 and 100. Two forms – Form A and B – were used: Form A was used for CELT 1 (April, 2001) and Form B was used for CELT 2 (January, 2002).

3.2.3. Procedures

The aim of Phase I was to obtain data on participants' listening proficiency, E/I, and use of LSs. The study participants were English department students who entered the college in April, 2001. Data on listening proficiency, personalities, and their LSs were gathered over a two-year period at the times deemed most appropriate and practical for each measure (Figure 6).

Letters of recruitment were delivered to second-year students by their course instructors asking potential participants to volunteer for this project on April 15, 2002 (Appendix D). The participants were told that the project included responding to questionnaires on personality (the MBTI), on LSs (revised SILL), and on their learning background (see Appendix C). They were also told to submit their listening test scores (the TOEIC and the CELT) that they had already taken at the beginning and end of their first year. The participants were assured that confidentiality would be strictly guaranteed.

56

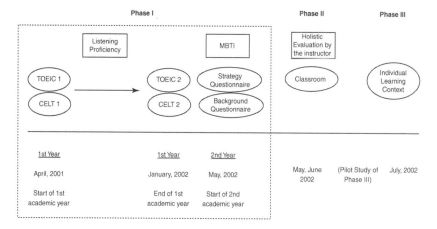

Figure 6. Procedures of the study.

The MBTI was administered to 147 participants on May 15, 2002 and the strategy and background questionnaires were given to 148 participants on May 22, 2002. The MBTI and questionnaires on LSs and their learning background were conducted when participants were in their second year of college, while the information on the development of listening proficiency is based on the TOEIC scores from their first year.

It was assumed that second-year students would be the best participants because they would have had time to successfully adjust to their new college life and studies. First-year students are busy with getting accustomed to college life after studying hard to pass the severe entrance exams: Among the new challenges they face at college are more classes with English native teachers (Nozaki 1993) and more communicative English classes. Furthermore, if first year students had been recruited, it is assumed that their self-reporting on LSs would consist primarily of strategies to pass the entrance exams.[8]

With respect to listening proficiency, as I will state in detail in the next section, a course teaching solely listening skills in the lan-

---

8   The wash-back effect of the entrance examination on the high school level of teaching English has been widely discussed (e.g., Brown/Yamashita 2000, Leonard 1998, Mulvey 2001), the influence on English learning and the choice of LSs are also assumed.

guage laboratory (LL) was required for all the first-year students, and it was expected that there would be a substantial development in their listening ability in the first year. In the second year, only elective listening courses are offered; therefore, I decided that the difference in scores between the tests at the beginning and at the end of the first year would give the fairest measure of the listening proficiency of all the students in the sample. Practically speaking, it was also desirable to have the listening test data before observing participants in the classroom and in the individual learning situations. Besides, participants' listening proficiency in January 2002 was assumed to be the same as that in May 2002 because February and March are the vacation months with no courses offered during this period of time.

The first TOEIC and CELT tests were administered respectively on April 5 and in the third week of April 2001 by my colleagues (Yasuyo Edasawa, Tsuyoshi Iida, Namie Saeki), and the second TOEIC and CELT tests were given on January 16 and in the third week of January 2002 respectively by the same colleagues.

As the nature of this study is descriptive, and not an intervention study to investigate the effect of specific strategy training, I judged that measurements of participants' listening proficiency did not have to be exactly concurrent with measurements of their E/I, LSs, and learning background.

3.3. Phase II

3.3.1. Objectives

I observed classes in order to confirm the results of the Phase I questionnaire data, and explore LSs that were difficult to identify through quantitative data collection.

58

3.3.2. Procedures

3.3.2.1. Pilot testing

To observe students' strategy use in class, two types of courses were considered as possibilities: (1) a course teaching solely listening skills in the LL given by Japanese instructors; and (2) an oral English (henceforth, OE) communication course teaching both speaking and listening skills given by native speakers of English in a normal classroom. Although in terms of focusing on listening, the former type of class seemed favorable, observable strategies would be severely restricted as the main interaction was between the participants and the machines. As mentioned before, the former type of class was required only for first-year students, and it was assumed that the second-year students were more appropriate for the goals of this study. On the other hand, in the OE course, students were expected to speak up as well as to understand what was communicated to them. To observe listening strategies, this type of course was thought to be more suitable because the instructors were all native speakers of English and consequently participants would have abundant opportunities to be exposed to English. Besides, this type of course was obligatory for all students for two years from their first year through second year, thus making it possible to have second-year students as participants in this study. The class size in the OE created favorable conditions for observation with a smaller number of students – fewer than 25; whereas the LL listening class had twice as many students as in the OE.

In order to pilot test the observation scheme, I attended five OE classes taught by Karen (pseudonym), a native English full-time professor of this college, on November 8, 15, and 22, and December 13 and 20 in 2001 with the informed consent of students and the teacher. Each class lasted for 90 minutes. All the OE classes had the same number of students, i.e., 20.

I set up the videotape in a corner of the classroom to record, and I focused my attention on how students used the social strategies in Table 4 in class.

Whether participants…	Description (When and how…)
1. ask instructor questions	
2. ask fellow students questions	
3. ask anyone to slow down	
4. ask anyone to repeat	
5. ask anyone to clarify or verify	

Table 4. Observation scheme.

The class size of 20 students in one class was not necessarily large compared to the usual English class size in Japan, but I discovered that students used very few strategies in the classroom. I tried to count the frequencies of such strategy use in one session, but by the end, the sheet was hardly ticked. This implied that Japanese learners of English use few observable strategies in a classroom situation and that additional methods to unveil less observable strategies would be needed because the observation scheme was able to detect only visible strategies. Therefore, the results of the pilot-testing led to the following change in method employed in Phase II; instead of relying on the observation scheme, the students' learning was described in field notes that would illustrate either their observable strategy use or lack of use in the classroom, and offer possible explanations for this behavior. It was assumed that use of field notes would highlight subtleties of behaviors.

3.3.2.2. The study

From the six instructors teaching the OE course, Tom (pseudonym) was selected because it was thought that he excelled in making the class more active. In support of this opinion, he had received outstanding course evaluations from students, and had a good reputation for being friendly to students. Tom was an experienced English instructor, who had finished his M.A. in the U.K., and had been teaching for more than ten years in colleges in the Kyoto area. Besides college teaching, he also worked as an actor performing English comedies with his colleague in Kyoto. It seemed certain that his talent as an actor contributed to making his class active and lively.

In May, the second recruitment letters (see Appendix E) were delivered through the course instructor requesting that the students who had participated in the Phase I study would allow their English class to be observed, to be videotaped, and to be interviewed at the end of the session. They were assured that their names would not be disclosed.

Thus, a preliminary observation was made on May 21, 2002, after receiving informed consent from both Tom and his students. The lesson plan of the class consisted broadly of two parts: a teacher-fronted part (TF) and a student-centered part (SC) such as pair or group activities. The TF included warm-ups in which Tom spoke for about five minutes to introduce the session, and explained the task to be undertaken in the session, and the students' presentation of their group activities. SC activities included speaking activities in pairs or groups. Four observations were made in total: May 28, June 4, June 11, and June 18.

In order to describe invisible strategy use and uncover the intentions of using strategies, a stimulated recall interview was conducted with two selected participants following the protocol of Gass and Mackey (2000). The interview was conducted in Japanese. After showing a ten-minute videotaped segment of the English class they had participated in, I asked participants to recall what they were thinking at that time, and attempted to elicit exactly what strategies they were using or trying to use. For the stimulated recall interview, two participants, Miki and Yuri, were chosen. The stimulated recall interview, which consisted of the showing of the videotape of the class, was conducted once on June 19 and focused on the session of June 18.[9] The video tape was taken to show both interviewees in the TF and SC activities for ten minutes respectively. In the stimulated recall interview, the videotape was paused in the following situations: (1) every two minutes; (2) when the participants showed some particular behavior such as embarrassed laughter; or (3) when they exhibited certain facial

---

9 It is recommended that stimulated recall interview be conducted as soon as the target activity is over to avoid memory decay. I tried to arrange the date as soon as the target session was over, but because of participants' course schedule, one day after the class was the earliest date.

expressions such as looking at a loss. I also asked participants to tell me to pause the videotape when they remembered something while they were watching the video. The stimulated recall session was scheduled for one day after the session was over. More information on Miki and Yuri will be presented in the next section.

The interview was conducted individually in a quiet room in the college so that the participants could feel comfortable and safe. In the interview, conducted in Japanese,[10] participants were told that the interview would not affect their course grades, and that their names would not be disclosed. After the stimulated recall interviews, they were asked additional questions concerning their background and their learning history based on the background questionnaire they had submitted.

3.3.3. Contexts and participants

In the field notes for this phase, both the general behavior of students in the classroom and that of specific students, i.e., of extroverts and introverts, were noted. In selecting which student behavior to observe, however, I encountered substantial difficulties. As revealed in Naiman et al.'s (1978/1996) study, students' personalities in the classroom could well be different from their natural in-born personalities detected by the personality questionnaires such as the EPI or the MBTI. The researchers revealed that their speculation about the extroversion and introversion of students based on classroom observation did not correspond to student scores of the EPI, and vice versa. To begin with, Tom was consulted about which students he thought were extroverted and introverted. According to a combination of the MBTI scores and the instructor's suggestions, I finally selected four participants for E/I respectively, which totaled eight students. From this pool of participants, I mainly focused on the most extroverted student (Miki) and the most introverted student (Yuri). They were selected as the main participants because each represented the extreme range of extroversion or introversion in the two observed classes; the converted MBTI scores

---

10   The interview transcripts were later translated into English (see Section 4.3.1).

(see Section 3.2.2.1) showing extroversion and introversion were 45 for Miki and 135 for Yuri (detailed information on the range of MBTI is shown in Table 8, and Figure 7). Another reason for their selection was that their English proficiency as assessed by the TOEIC was approximately the same, as shown in Table 5.

Name	E/I	MBTI scrores	MBTI IP	TOEIC scores	
				Listening	Reading
Miki	Extrovert	45	Clear	285	195
Yuri	Introvert	135	Clear	290	210

Table 5. Profile of the two participants. (The range of the TOEIC scores is shown in Table 9. The criteria of MBTI-IP are explained in Table 3.)

3.4. Phase III

3.4.1. Contexts and participants

Miki and Yuri were also selected to be participants in Phase III.

3.4.2. Tasks

To triangulate the findings of Phase I, and to observe participants' strategy use in an individual learning situation, two types of tasks were designed which will become clear below. They each had a similar design and the materials were pitched at a similar intellectual level, except that Task B allowed for the possibility of interaction. The two tasks were pilot tested for their procedures with three third-year student volunteers of the same college on June 25, 2002.

In task Type A, participants were asked to listen to a tape (cf. Appendix F), which was less than one-minute long, of a monologue by one person about her new friend. Participants were given five minutes to listen to the tape, during which time they were freely able to stop, rewind, and forward the tape. They were asked to write down in English as much information as they could comprehend. Besides manipulating the tape recorder, they were also able to use references such as English monolingual, bilingual, and electronic dictionaries, which were made available to them.

In task Type B, participants were asked to sit with a native speaker of English, and to listen to him/her reading aloud a transcript (cf. Appendix G) of one person talking about his new friend. Type B task was designed in exactly the same way as Type A task so that a direct comparison between them could easily be made. The amount of information in the transcript, and the speed of the two speeches were almost the same. Just as participants were allowed to freely interact with the tape in task Type A, in task Type B they were told that they could ask the reader any questions at any time. Reference sources such as English monolingual, bilingual, and electronic dictionaries were equally made available for task Type B.

Task Type A and Type B were administered to students individually on different dates: initially I gave the Type A task (July 16, 2002), followed a week later by the Type B task (July 23, 2002). It was felt that this interval was necessary so that the participants would not confuse the two types of tasks.

3.4.3. Stimulated recall interviews

In order to describe less visible strategy use and to uncover the intentions underlying the use of strategies, I applied a stimulated recall interview to two selected participants (Miki and Yuri) following Gass and Mackey (2000). While showing participants the five-minute long videotapes of the activities they used to complete Task A and Task B immediately following each task, I asked them to recall what they were thinking at that time, and what strategies they were using or trying to use. In the stimulated recall interviews, the videotape was paused in the following situations: (1) every thirty seconds; (2) when the participants showed some particular behavior; (3) when I noticed expressions of interest or emotion on their faces. I also asked participants to tell me to pause the videotape when they remembered what they were thinking while they were watching the video. The interview was conducted in Japanese and its transcript was later translated into English (see Sections 4.4.2 and 4.4.4).

3.4.4. Procedures

The purpose of providing tasks was to triangulate the findings of Phases I and II, and to identify the impact of E/I in an individual learning context. In June, I delivered the third recruitment letter (see Appendix H) asking Miki and Yuri if they would participate in a task session, in which they would complete two kinds of tasks on different dates. The letter also stated that I would observe their sessions, and videotape and interview each of them after the session. They were told that their names would not be disclosed.

With their informed consent, I conducted task sessions of the two kinds of tasks: Task A on July 12 and Task B on July 19.

3.5. Summary of methodologies

The research methods used in this study are summarized in Table 6.

Type of data	Instrument	Source and date	Number of participants
Quantitative Phase I Data sets	TOEIC listening section TOEIC 1 TOEIC 2	TOEIC April 2001 January 2002	132 132
	CELT listening section CELT 1 (Form A) CELT 2 (Form B)	McGraw Hill 2000 April 2001 January 2002	126 124
	MBTI Form G (Japanese edition)	Association for Psychological Type May 2002	147
	Strategy questionnaire (Revised SILL)	Adapted from SILL (Oxford 1990) May 2002	148
	Background questionnaire	Adapted from SILL (Oxford 1990) May 2002	148
Qualitative Phase II Data sets	Classroom observation (field notes)	Developed for this study – May and June 2002	44
	Stimulated recall interviews	Gass and Mackey 2000 – June 2002	2
	Course instructor's holistic evaluation of participants' personality types	Developed for this study – May 2002	38
Qualitative Phase III Data sets	Tape-listening task (Task A)	Developed for this study – May 2002	2
	Stimulated recall interviews	Gass and Mackey 2000 – July 2002	2
	Interactive listening task (Task B)	Developed for this study – July 2002	2
	Stimulated recall interviews	Gass and Mackey 2000 – July 2002	2

Table 6. Research methodologies.

4.   Results

4.1. Introduction

This chapter summarizes the results of Phase I (a survey-based study), Phase II (a classroom-based study), and Phase III (a task implementation case study). Each phase was designed to explore the three research themes: (1) to describe the characteristic strategies of Japanese learners of English in an EFL context; (2) to identify the characteristic strategies of extroverts and introverts in an EFL context; and (3) to observe whether E/I have an impact on EFL proficiency, in particular on listening proficiency. First, the results of the Phase I quantitative study will be presented.

4.2. Phase I: Quantitative study

4.2.1. Distributions of E/I

Table 7 shows the distribution of extroverted and introverted participants[11] based on the MBTI.

Preference scores (PSs) indicate how clearly E/I is manifested by participants. The distribution of E/I demonstrates that, for example, ten participants were very clearly disposed to extroversion, while two were clearly disposed to introversion. Although Japanese people are often assumed to be introverted (see Section 2.2.1), a surprising 67.7%

---

11   One participant missed taking the MBTI, and 14 students who had lived abroad for one year or more were eliminated from the analysis. The number of participants used for the analysis is therefore 133.

of all participants showed an inclination to extroversion, though the degree of that tendency varied.

Indication of preference (IP)		Extroverts		Introverts	
Criteria	Score range	n	%	n	%
Sight preference	1-9	15	11.3	10	7.5
Moderate preference	11-19	19	14.3	8	6.0
Clear preference	21-49	46	34.6	23	17.3
Very clear preference	51-	10	7.5	2	1.5
Total		90	67.7	43	32.3

Table 7. Distribution of E/I by indication of preference (N = 133).

Although the MBTI yields dichotomous information, the information can be converted into an interval scale (see Section 3.2.2.1). Table 7 presents descriptive statistics for the extroversion/introversion by indication of preference, and Table 8 shows the descriptive statistics for continuous numbers of extroversion/introversion.

Max	Min	M	SD	Skewness	Kurtosis
161	39	88.71	29.57	0.38	-0.72

Table 8. Descriptive statistics for continuous numbers of E/I (N=133; Extroversion ranges below 100; Introversion ranges above 100).

While the mean value was in the direction of extroverts (the theoretical mid-point being 100), values for skewness and kurtosis were within the accepted limits. Figure 7 shows that extroversion and introversion were almost normally distributed.

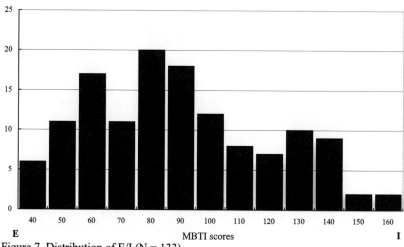

E   MBTI scores   I

Figure 7. Distribution of E/I (N = 133).

4.2.2. Distributions of listening proficiency

Table 9 presents descriptive statistics for the listening proficiency of all participants in terms of the TOEIC and the CELT test scores.

Listening proficiency tests	Range	Max	Min	N	SD	Skew- ness	Kur- tosis
TOEIC 1 (April 2001)	250	355	105	214.4	47.3	0.15	-0.06
TOEIC 2 (January 2002)	245	385	140	266.6	54.0	-0.15	-0.65
CELT 1 (April 2001)	64	72	8	48.2	11.4	-0.55	0.73
CELT 2 (January 2002)	48	78	30	53.0	10.0	0.01	-0.19

Table 9. Descriptive statistics for listening proficiency tests (N = 132 for TOEIC 1 and 2; N = 126 for CELT 1; and N = 124 for CELT 2. Form A was used for CELT 1 and Form B for CELT 2).

The maximum score possible for the TOEIC listening section is 495, and 100 for CELT. The mean value of the TOEIC in April 2001 shows

69

participants' listening proficiency when first entering college. It can be seen that studying for one academic year (from April 2001 through January 2002) improved their listening ability by 52 points on average. The scores were normally distributed with the accepted limit of skewness and kurtosis. The same tendency can be observed in the listening scores of the CELT. Participants gained 4.7 points on average from April through January.

4.2.3. Distributions of LS

4.2.3.1. Distributions of LS by modes

LSs can be divided into several subcategories as explained in Chapter 2. For example, Oxford (1990) adopted six subscales while O'Malley and Chamot (1990) used three. Although a striking difference seems to exist between those two, they are actually closely related except in the case of communication strategies; memory strategies can be assumed to constitute one specific type of cognitive strategies (e.g., Dörnyei/ Skehan 2003, Takeuchi 2003b), and affective strategies and social strategies can be combined. Here, the four modes will be employed as explained before: cognitive, metacognitive, communication, and socio-affective strategies. Table 10 presents the descriptive statistics for the four dimensions of the four modes (subscales): strategy use, strategy preferences, strategy helpfulness, and previous strategy use (see Section 3.2.2.3).

As shown in Table 10, with regard to strategy use, the mean value for the communication subscale was the highest (3.17), and for the cognitive subscale (2.79), the lowest. Regarding strategy preferences, as shown in Table 10, the highest mean value is 3.53 (metacognitive strategies), and the lowest is 3.27 (communication strategies). Overall, the mean values of helpfulness in all four modes were high.

Modes/ Dimensions	M	Mdn	Mode	SD	Max	Min	Skew- ness	Kur- tosis
Cognitive								
Use	2.79	2.76	2.62	0.43	3.90	1.71	0.33	0.20
Preferences	3.48	3.48	3.48	0.45	4.67	2.14	-0.08	0.42
Helpfulness	3.87	3.86	3.90	0.39	4.68	2.67	0.03	-0.24
Previous use	2.94	2.93	3.10	0.42	4.10	2.00	0.18	-0.27
Communication								
Use	3.17	3.23	3.23	0.55	4.54	1.62	-0.23	-0.11
Preferences	3.27	3.23	3.08	0.40	4.31	2.08	0.04	0.29
Helpfulness	3.58	3.62	3.62	0.45	4.85	2.46	-0.02	-0.17
Previous use	3.00	3.00	3.23	0.59	4.54	1.38	-0.12	-0.17
Metacognitive								
Use	2.94	2.93	2.93	0.56	4.57	1.57	0.04	0.04
Preferences	3.53	3.54	3.86	0.48	5.00	2.21	0.20	0.3
Helpfulness	4.05	4.04	3.86	0.48	5.00	2.86	-0.07	-0.59
Previous use	2.94	2.93	2.71	0.60	4.79	1.43	0.14	0.05
Socio-affective								
Use	3.08	3.08	2.77	0.57	4.15	1.62	-0.21	-0.44
Preferences	3.50	3.54	3.62	0.52	5.00	2.38	0.21	-0.04
Helpfulness	3.93	3.96	3.77	0.48	5.00	2.77	0.06	-0.50
Previous use	2.92	2.92	2.92	0.63	4.62	1.54	0.02	-0.21

Table 10. Descriptive statistics for LS (N=134; the possible ranges are from 1 to 5 scale points).

Although the mean values for previous strategy use generally corresponded to strategy use mean values, Figure 8 charts an interesting comparison among the four dimensions of the four types of LSs (modes): 'use', 'previous use', 'preferences', and 'helpfulness' of LSs. As the graph (Figure 8) indicates, we do not see a major gap between previous and present use of metacognitive strategies, but can find a difference in cognitive, communication and socio-affective strategies. In regard to cognitive strategies, participants used them less frequently than in the past; in contrast, they made more use of communication and socio-affective strategies compared to the past. This will be discussed in Chapter 5.

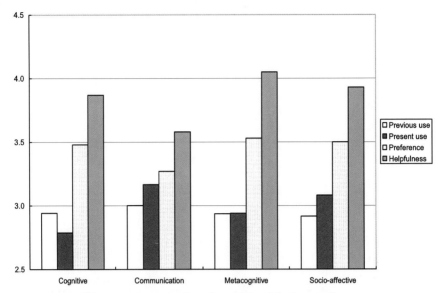

Figure 8. Differences among the four dimensions of the four modes.

4.2.3.2. Distributions of individual LS

Distributions for some of the individual items are shown in Tables 11 and 12.

Strategies	Mode	Min	Max	M	SD
Using references	Cognitive	2	5	4.75	0.58
Guessing	Communication	1	5	4.10	0.95
Using synonyms	Communication	2	5	4.05	0.83
Using gestures	Communication	1	5	3.96	0.99
Learning from own mistakes	Metacognitive	2	5	3.90	0.93
Learning culture	Socio-affective	1	5	3.85	1.02
Long-term objectives	Metacognitive	1	5	3.84	1.00
Request to repeat	Socio-affective	1	5	3.83	1.07
Rewarding oneself	Socio-affective	1	5	3.81	1.21
Self-evaluation	Metacognitive	1	5	3.75	0.88

Table 11. Most frequently used strategies by all students (N=134).

The questionnaire contained 61 strategies. As shown in Table 11, using support references (cognitive strategies) such as consulting electronic

72

dictionaries was the most frequently used strategy among Japanese college students. Strategies used in conversation rated high: for example, guessing the meaning and using gestures or synonyms when students could not communicate well. Metacognitive strategies such as learning from their own mistakes, setting objectives to learn English, and self-assessment of their improvement were also often used. Giving themselves a reward when they did well, asking the interlocutor to repeat when they were unable to understand, and learning the target culture, three socio-affective strategies, were also frequently present.

On the other hand, the least frequently used strategies are shown in Table 12. The two least common strategies – attending out-of-class events (cognitive strategies) or thinking in English (cognitive strategies) – might be rather difficult to employ in an EFL context as compared to an ESL context because such events are usually rare in the former, learners of English having little cause to think in English because they can communicate in their own language in daily life.

Strategies	Mode	Min	Max	M	SD
Participating in out-of-class events	Cognitive	1	5	1.57	1.02
Thinking in English	Cognitive	1	4	1.58	0.78
Physically acting out new words	Cognitive	1	5	1.61	0.95
Keeping a diary	Socio-affective	1	5	1.68	1.05
Finding a conversional partner	Metacognitive	1	5	1.78	0.97
Using the Internet	Cognitive	1	5	1.89	1.11
Intensive learning	Metacognitive	1	5	2.03	1.08
Spiral review	Metacognitive	1	5	2.11	0.91
Reading for pleasure	Cognitive	1	5	2.12	0.95
Making up new words	Communication	1	5	2.15	1.17

Table 12. Least frequently used strategies by all students (N =134).

As was also reported in previous studies (Takeuchi 1993, 2003b), keeping a language learning diary (socio-affective strategies) was an infrequent option. Interestingly, use of the Internet in English (cognitive strategies) was not popular among college students. The college the participants attended offered a convenient Internet service with fast access for all students. If students had wished to use the Internet for language learning, they could easily have done so. For Japanese learners of English, physically acting out a word or phrase (cognitive strategies) in order to understand or remember it, or indeed utilizing a new word, is difficult because of cultural values; in other words, Japanese learners on the whole are not accustomed to expressing ideas with gestures or able to narrow the distance between their native and target language by taking risks with new lexical items in an educational setting.

4.2.4. Reliabilities

4.2.4.1. Reliabilities of the strategy questionnaire

Table 13 presents the internal consistency reliability, which was measured using Cronbach's alpha for the LS questionnaire, in terms of all the items (61 in total) and the four dimensions (use, helpfulness, preferences, and previous use) for the four modes (cognitive, communication, metacognitive, and socio-affective strategies).

In general, the reliabilities of the LS questionnaire were high. The all-item analysis shows that their reliabilities for all four dimensions were more than .90, and the reliability of each mode ranges from a low .69 for preferences of communication strategies to a high .84 for helpfulness of metacognitive strategies.

LS dimensions	Cognitive (21)	Communi- cation(13)	Metacognitive (14 items)	Socio- Affective (13)	Items (61)
Use	0.749	0.735	0.803	0.765	0.910
Helpfulness	0.805	0.752	0.847	0.816	0.922
Preferences	0.781	0.697	0.780	0.812	0.918
Previous use	0.747	0.759	0.821	0.814	0.918

Table 13. Reliabilities (Cronbach's alpha) of the LS questionnaire (N= 133).

4.2.4.2. The relationship between the MBTI results and the instructor's holistic evaluation

To triangulate the MBTI results, the Pearson correlation coefficient between the MBTI E/I values (PSs being converted into continuous numbers) with the seven-scale instructor's holistic evaluation of learners' E/I was calculated; the result indicated a statistically significant correlation ($r = .557$; $p < .001$; n = 38). Figure 9 presents the distribution between the two values. In general, the lower the course instructor's holistic evaluation, the lower the MBTI scores were, and vice versa. That is, the MBTI/pencil and paper questionnaire results generally corresponded with the course instructor's intuitive assessment of learners.

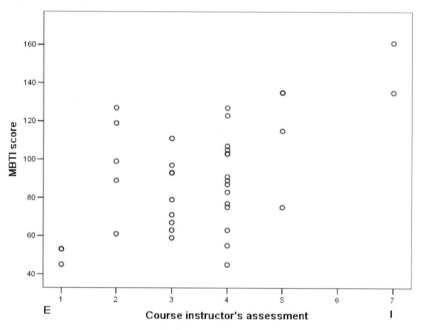

Figure 9. The relationship between the MBTI and the instructor's holistic evaluation (n = 38 Ss in observed classes; each dot represents an individual student).

However, Figure 9 also shows discrepancies between the MBTI scores and the course instructor's holistic evaluation of the 38 students in the two classes I observed. For example, students considered to be mid-range by the course instructor's assessment – four points on the X axis – had varied MBTI scores; or participants scoring as introverted (n = 3) and extroverted (n = 1) on the MBTI appeared to have opposite characteristics in the classroom. Similar discrepancies were also reported in Naiman *et al.* (1978/1996).

4.2.5. Impacts of E/I on LS

As is usual in the case where there are several independent and dependent variables, in order to investigate the impact of extroversion/introversion on LSs, a one-way multivariate analysis of variance (MANOVA) was carried out on four subscales: The dependent variables were the four dimensions – strategy use, helpfulness, previous strategy use and preferences – as mentioned before. For the MANOVA, participants showing clear and very clear preferences in their PS were selected for the analysis: Es = 56, Is = 25, and the total number of participants equaled 81 out of the entire sample of 133 participants. This is because within the distribution of extroversion and introversion, a variation in the PSs was observed (see Table 7 and Figure 7), such that PS of slight or moderate clearness involves the possibility of showing the opposite personality (Chapter 3). As previously stated (see Section 3.2.2.1), the E/I of respondents with 'moderate' or 'slight' preferences may not appear clearly, and including respondents with moderate or slight preferences would make it difficult to reveal conclusively the impact of E/I on foreign language learning. Type I error[12] level was set at $p < .05$.

4.2.5.1. Impacts of E/I on cognitive strategies

A one-way MANOVA was performed on the cognitive strategies. In the multivariate level, no significant main effect of E/I, Pillai's = 0.104, F $(4,76)$ = 2.20, p = .08, was observed, though this can be assumed to be a trend toward statistical significance because the type I error level was below .10.

4.2.5.2. Impacts of E/I on communication strategies

In the same way, a one-way MANOVA was applied to the communication strategies, which also produced no significant main effect on E/I (Pillai's = 0.066).

---

12   Type I error means "the researcher concludes that a treatment does have an effect when in fact the treatment has no effect" (Gravetter/Wallnau 1999: 195).

4.2.5.3. Impacts of E/I on metacognitive strategies

A one-way MANOVA was conducted on metacognitive strategies. At the multivariate level, the main effect of E/I, Pillai's = 0.115 was nearly significant, F (4, 76) = 2.47, p = .052. At the univariate level, a significant main effect of E/I was observed on strategy preferences. For the univariate level, the type I error level was set at $p < .013$ (.05/4 = .0125) unless otherwise mentioned. This is because setting alpha at p = .05 will increase the danger of causing type I error. The analysis of variance (ANOVA) results, with all means for metacognitive strategies, are summarized in Table 14.

Dimensions	Mean		df	F	p
	E (n=56)	I (n=25)			
Use	3.05	2.71	(1, 79)	6.53	0.013
Helpfulness	4.10	3.98	(1, 79)	1.05	0.308
Preferences	3.64	3.33	(1, 79)	9.11	0.003*
Previous use	3.05	2.72	(1, 79)	5.29	0.024

Table 14. The differences between E/I in metacognitive strategies (*$p < .013$).

Table 14 shows significant differences between extroverts and intro-verts in their preferences for metacognitive strategies, indicating that extroverts' scores were significantly higher than introverts'.

4.2.5.4. Impacts of E/I on socio-affective strategies

Finally, I applied a one-way MANOVA to socio-affective strategies. At the multivariate level, a significant main effect of E/I, Pillai's = 0.180, F (4, 76) = 4.17, $p < .004$ was observed. At the univariate level, a significant main effect of E/I was observed on strategy use, previous strategy use, and preferences. The findings are summarized in Table 15.

Dimensions	Mean		df	F	p
	E (n=56)	I (n=25)			
Use	3.19	2.82	(1, 79)	7.82	0.006*
Helpfulness	3.96	3.84	(1, 79)	1.08	0.303
Preferences	3.62	3.23	(1, 79)	12.43	0.001*
Previous use	3.06	2.59	(1, 79)	10.08	0.002*

Table 15. The differences between E/I in socio-affective strategies (*$p < .013$).

Table 15 indicates significant differences between extroverts and introerts in their use, preferences, and previous strategy use of socio-affective strategies. As observed in the case of metacognitive strategies, the scores of Es were significantly higher than Is' in all three dimensions.

The analysis employing the MANOVA points to the fact that among the four subscales of the LS questionnaire, metacognitive and socio-affective strategies were the groups of strategies on which the E/I variable has the most impact. This result will be triangulated in the Phase II and Phase III analyses.

4.2.5.5. Impacts of E/I on individual strategies

Although the analysis of questionnaire data by modes (cognitive, communication, metacognitive, socio-affective) did not yield any characteristic LSs of Is, in terms of individual LSs, some strategies were found to be frequently used by Is (Table 16).

As indicated in Table 16, two LSs were frequently used by Is and Es: requesting to repeat (socio-affective) and strategies to utilize grammatical knowledge (cognitive) were frequently used by Is; praising oneself (socio-affective), and nodding (communication) were frequently used by Es. The most noteworthy strategy uncovered in Table 16 was the use of grammatical knowledge of Is. One interpretation is that Is intentionally used grammatical knowledge for listening comprehension. Compared to reading or writing skills, the scope of using grammatical knowledge is smaller because time for decoding information using grammatical knowledge is limited, but learners can use such deductive reasoning strategies to precisely understand what was said.

Rank	Extroverts	Mean (n=56)	Introverts	Mean (n=25)
1	Using references	4.71	Using references	4.84
2	Guessing	4.23	Guessing	4.24
3	Using synonyms	4.16	Using synonyms	4.04
4	Using gestures	4.14	*Asking to repeat*	*3.92 (3.75)*
5	*Praising oneself*	*4.07 (3.40)*	Using gestures	3.92
6	Noticing one's errors	3.98	Noticing one's errors	3.80
7	Self-evaluation	3.95	Learning culture	3.72
8	Learning culture	3.93	*Using grammatical information*	*3.67 (3.45)*
9	Long term objectives	3.91	Long term objectives	3.64
10	*Nodding*	*3.91 (3.52)*	Self-evaluation	3.60

Table 16. Most frequently used LSs by E/I (Strategies in italics indicate the differences between Es and Is; the parenthesis shows the mean of LS of the opposite type, e.g., while the mean of 'praising oneself' of extroverts was 4.07, that of introverts was 3.40).

4.2.6. Impacts of E/I on listening proficiency

One of the research questions of this study was to observe the impact of E/I on listening proficiency. For this purpose, two sources of information about listening proficiency were analyzed: the TOEIC test scores, and the CELT test scores.

4.2.6.1. Impacts of E/I on the TOEIC test scores

Participants sat for the test twice: in April 2001 when first enrolled at the college, and in January 2002 after attending the university for one academic year. For this purpose, I applied a repeated analysis of variance (ANOVA) to the same participants, though the number of participants is slightly different because of absences (n = 79: n (I) = 25; n (E) = 54). A repeated ANOVA yielded no significant results: the Pillai's Trace = 0.028, F (1, 77) = 2.18, p = .14. However, the mean scores of the Es were higher than those of the Is initially, and the Is appeared to be catching up with the Es after studying for almost one academic year (Figure 10).

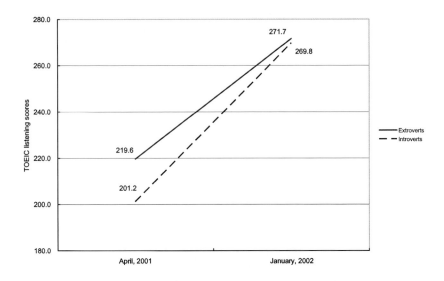

Figure 10. Improvement of the TOEIC scores by E/I.

The same tendencies can be seen in the development of the CELT scores (Figure 11).

4.2.6.2. Impacts of E/I on the CELT test scores

Participants also had opportunities to take the CELT test twice (in April 2001 and January 2002) as a course requirement of the LL listening course (see Chapter 3). As a result of a repeated ANOVA with the same procedures as the TOEIC, no significant results were observed: results as follows – the Pillai's Trace = 0.004, F (1, 70) = 0.31, and p = .58. As with the TOEIC, the mean value of the Es was rather higher than that of the Is, and after one year of study at the college, the Is seemed to draw almost level with the Es.

80

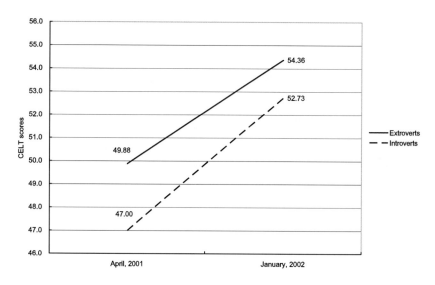

Figure 11. Improvements of the CELT scores by E/I.

4.2.7. Summary of Phase I

The analysis applying repeated ANOVA points to the fact that there were no significant interactions between the TOEIC scores and E/I, or between the CELT scores and E/I. While correlations between LSs and E/I were observed, there is the question of why an interaction between E/I and listening proficiency was not observed. Although the interaction was not statistically significant, in the beginning the scores of the Es were higher than the Is on both the TOEIC and the CELT, and after one year of English study at the college, the gaps between Es and Is were reduced – that is, the improvements of Is were greater than those of Es. This will be discussed in the next chapter.

4.3. Phase II: LS use in the classroom

4.3.1. Observations and stimulated recall interview

The two main objectives of observing classes were to confirm the results of the questionnaire data, and to pilot test the observation scheme. I found the observation scheme less useful than open-ended field notes, so I decided not to use a formal observation scheme. I chose to describe the students' learning in field notes to illustrate the students' strategy use or the lack of it in the classroom, and offer possible explanations for their behavior (see Section 3.3.2.1). Each session lasted 90 minutes, and I observed four sessions in total.

4.3.1.1. Strategy use in teacher-fronted (TF) portions of the class

In Tom's classes, various kinds of activities were used, and the analysis based on my field notes indicated that it would be useful to distinguish those activities in terms of teacher-fronted (TF) and student-centered (SC) components. Followings are selected excerpts[13] from my field notes on the three types of input from the teacher, and the stimulated recall interview results related to those situations. In the TF part of the class, students had chances to listen to different types of input: (1) short stories by Tom that were told as warm-ups; (2) explanations of tasks in class; and (3) instructions concerning class tasks or home assignments.

> *May 28, 2002*
> The majority of the participants assembled five or ten minutes before the commencement of the session, three of them arriving only just in time. They sat in two rows on moveable chairs, each with a small table. The OE class was conducted in a classroom where students could move their chairs anytime to form pairs or groups of five or six students. Tom entered the classroom a fraction late with a smile on his face saying "good afternoon" and awaiting the response from the students. He took the attendance register by calling out students' family names. Generally students replied in a vaguely audible voice, saying "Yes," or "Here," with some students raising their hand and some just

---

13   I chose the field notes based on typical scenes.

replying vocally. Twenty-two students were present while two students were absent. The atmosphere in the classroom was calm and silent. After checking the attendance, Tom explained the objectives and procedures of that day. The topic was how to use rejoinders, "Really?" "No!" and "No kidding". Without explicitly presenting these terms, he first tried to elicit these expressions from students. Tom first introduced them in Japanese saying *Uso* or *Majide* (Really) in a funny voice, which brought laughter from students. Although Tom posed questions about other expressions, nobody dared to answer.

Getting little response, Tom quickly told students to discuss these expressions with their neighbors. Students murmured to each other for about 30 seconds. While waiting for the answer, Tom was walking around the blackboard and entertaining students by uttering other similar Japanese words, although he did not usually speak Japanese in the classroom. Tom always had a smile on his face, and some, though not all, students also had smiles on their faces. I thought the atmosphere of the classroom was soft and relaxed. Then quite abruptly, Tom pointed to one student to respond to his words, "I found 1000 yen on the street," and she replied tentatively with the correct answer: "Really?" While writing it on the blackboard, he also introduced another expression "No!" Tom urged students to repeat these with several different intonations. He then pointed to other students to elicit other similar expressions: "Are you serious?" or "Are you joking?" Students could have answered voluntarily, which was what Tom appeared to be expecting, but there were no volunteers and all the remarks occurred only when students were called on by Tom. However, they did know the answer because they were able to answer when called on. They just did not volunteer any answers whatsoever.

It became quickly apparent also that students did not ask questions when they did not understand the instructor's directions. For example, Tom told students to form a group of four students around an empty chair for an activity; saying "Okay, I will put you in a group of four. I want you to sit around the empty chair". When it came to students actually moving their chairs to form a group, Tom realized that none of the groups had put an empty chair in the middle of their circle. He needed to emphasize and repeat, the instruction "sit around an empty chair". Two groups out of the five understood Tom's directions and brought an empty chair, but the other three groups were still wondering what the problem was and watching what other groups were doing. It was clear that even at this stage no single student asked Tom what they were meant to do. The simple understanding of the instructions given by Tom was not easy for students. "In today's activity," Tom said to students after distributing small pieces of paper clipped together, "Take off the clip, spread the papers out and put them face down". Tom's gestures helped students understand Tom's intentions, especially about placing the items face down. However, it seemed that the expression "spread the papers out" was not easily grasped by some students. In fact, several students attempted to compensate for their lack of understanding by watching what other groups were doing. Although the students could have asked questions, at no time did the students ask any questions. This is assumed to be representative of typical Japanese classroom culture.

June 4, 2002

As in the previous session, Tom entered the classroom with a smile on his face, and called the names of students one by one while he marked them present in his notebook. After that Tom said "Okay" and started to relate a recent incident in his life. His story was as follows:

He had been living with his roommate in Japanese style housing in Kyoto, Japan for nearly five years when one morning he was woken up unusually early by something strange touching him. To his shock he discovered a worm crawling on his throat and called out in a disgusted voice.

His story was accompanied by both hand gestures and facial expressions, and he was successful in attracting the students' interest. Every student was magnetized by Tom's face and seemed to be stimulated by his story. They were listening intently with smiles, and occasionally broke into laughter. He also talked about a problem he had had with his neighbors about taking out the garbage. His monologue went on for nearly ten minutes. It was like watching TV. Nobody interrupted his performance or attempted to ask questions.

Because this was obviously a warm-up routine, students might not have been used to interrupting or posing questions. Furthermore, because Tom was addressing the students as a group, not as individuals, they clearly did not feel the necessity to respond individually to his story. In spite of that, the apparently reserved attitude of students was an interesting and symbolic phenomenon.

June 11, 2002

At the end of the session today, Tom announced the assignment for the next session. He wanted students to read a newspaper article about a Japanese man traveling around the world, compose some questions about it and answer them on B5-size paper in a bullet style. The article was sufficiently interesting to simulate questions because the man traveled by bicycle and asked his company for a one-year leave of absence for his trip. Observing students listening to Tom's instructions, it became evident that they did not understand their assignment for the following week. They displayed anxiety in their facial expressions and asked each other about the assignment in Japanese. The terms "B5 paper" or "bullet style" must have been particularly difficult to understand because they could not even guess what was meant, and in addition, the connection between the questions and the answers was not clear to them. They did not know what they actually needed to do by the following week. Their coping strategies were closely observed at this point. Nobody asked questions to clarify the assignment. It seemed that Tom also did not realize that students did not understand what he had assigned as homework. In a few minutes, a buzzer signaling the end of the lesson rang and students left the classroom continuing to ask each other about the assignment.

When several students were questioned after the lesson, the general impression was that they had not understood the assigned homework. Indeed, three students approached the observer and asked about the meaning of "B5 paper" and "bullet style", and whether or not they should write comments on their own questions. When asked why they had not clarified the assignment with Tom, three students mentioned that they did not feel comfortable asking Tom, and that they preferred to ask their friends.

This was a significant moment in observing and analyzing the behavior of Japanese learners of English in the classroom. They did not ask questions in English even when they needed to. They preferred to ask each other or the Japanese researcher. This phenomenon will be discussed in more detail in Chapter 5.

4.3.1.2. Strategy use in student-centered (SC) portions of the class

In the SC part of the lesson, students were engaged in pair or group activities. My field notes summarizing these activities are as follows:

June 11, 2002
In the group activity, students were engaged in a game, in which they would ask and answer what they were doing at a particular time described by a card they were given. In groups of four, which Tom randomly formed, students picked up either a "time card" or "action card". The time cards were easy for students since they had specific times such as "two thirty in the morning" or "seven at night," but the action cards were often difficult to express in English because the students did not know how to explain the actions depicted on the cards. It was observed that they invariably chose to solve that problem by asking their friends in their native language, or referring to their electronic dictionary, which almost all the students owned.[14] However, students seemed to be enjoying the group activity; loud voices and cheerful laughter filled the classroom. Meanwhile, Tom moved among all the groups and suggested better expressions or asked them questions. But at no time did any student initiate a question for the instructor. All of the questions were posed by the instructor. In this sense, the interaction between students and Tom was one-way. Given this behavior it might be that students may not be able to solve problems alone. Tom did not necessarily come and help them just when they needed him, so it was curious that they did not raise their hand to summon him.

---

14   The informal survey in two classes found no students who did not own electronic dictionaries.

In this part of the session – small group activities – the use of various LSs might be expected. However, when students needed to use the LSs, they switched to their native tongue and asked each other in order to overcome the obstacles. In this sense, they used many socio-affective strategies: asking questions to fellow students to clarify or verify, but they used them in Japanese. It is probable that this is because this was a mono-lingual native-speaker group, i.e., Japanese.

June 18, 2002

In the group activity, students were working in groups of four, which consisted of different members from the last session. The task was to practice the functions of explaining national customs and asking each other questions based on comparisons among Iranian, Thai, and Japanese customs. Students were given a text to read and asked to write down the similarities and the differences among the three cultures. Tom told the students that they should not be silent; that they were required to offer some comments on other people's remarks. For that purpose, Tom put some useful and necessary expressions on the blackboard such as "My idea was similar," "I wrote the same thing," "I agree with you, but I have a different example". He emphasized that casual conversation was different from formal speech and they could talk freely.

How students interacted with each other and with Tom was the focus of observation. At first, students were looking down at their own notes and just reading without making eye contact with each other, but as time went on they began to talk while making eye contact. During the task, Tom walked around the classroom, encouraging students to speak up or giving suggestions to each group. In time he found a group in which students were merely reading their notes and failing to react to each other. He quickly encouraged them to engage with each other, indicating that they should utilize the useful expressions on the blackboard. When Tom heard an inappropriate expression, he corrected it; for example, Tom told one student to use "Once more" instead of "One more". This task continued for about 15 minutes. As in the last session, it was always Tom who asked questions or offered suggestions. Even when he was attending to a particular group, the members listened to him and did not ask questions or say anything to him.

However, Miki's group behaved a little differently. Miki made eye contact with Tom without saying anything and asked questions in the following interchange.

Miki: Iranian...
Tom: Why do Iranian...
Miki: Why do Iranian... having no (*naino* in Japanese)...? [using gestures trying to show something, and asking her friend for help] Why do Iranians wear short sleeves?

Tom: Because if they show the body, it's uh too sexually attractive for men. So you should only show your body to your husband.

Miki: Oh, I see, thank you.

Tom: But, you know, lots of Arab women, uh, especially the ones who have lived in the West, in England and so on, underneath the veil, they wear very expensive Chanel suits, jewelry, makeup and everything. Underneath.

Miki: They wear various things [in Japanese].

Tom: Right. At home they wear very high fashion, and so on. So just the same. But they cannot show it outside the house. Sometimes, uh, western women visit an Arabic house and are very surprised. They see makeup. Oh, my God. And the Arabs say "we are women, same as you". But they cannot show it outside the house. That's the difference. That's the different point.

While Tom was responding to Miki, the other three members in her group also received the benefit of listening to Tom's explanation; however, students in other groups did not pay attention to him although Tom was talking in a loud voice. He did not repeat the same explanation to the whole class, although other students got a chance to listen to that story when each group summarized its discussion at the end of the session. Despite the fact that the groups that day were randomly decided, the group that Miki joined was active, while Yuri's group was not active. Tom gave suggestions and corrections about English usage to Yuri's group, but did not provide a story as he did with Miki's group. When Tom had finished his story and tried to move on from Miki's group, he returned and added something, which was inaudible. Tom visited Miki's group more often and stayed there longer than other groups. Miki was successful in eliciting interesting stories for her group from the course instructor.

This part of the session was significant in observing Miki's (E) use of socio-affective strategies. She successfully interacted with Tom during the student-centered (SC) components, which encouraged more input from the instructor. It is also interesting that he stayed longer with and visited this group more frequently.

4.3.1.3. Stimulated recall interview with Miki and Yuri

Regarding the above situation when Miki was talking with Tom, both Miki (E) and Yuri (I) were later asked to recall what they were thinking following the stimulated recall interview procedure. The transcript of the interview with Miki (E) will be presented first.

Interviewer: Tom came to your group in this scene. Did you ask him to come?
Miki: I don't know why he came to us.
Interviewer: Do you often ask Tom for help?
Miki: I think that occasionally I might call him to talk or ask questions, but I don't remember well. I don't know why, but he often comes to my group.
Interviewer: Do you like talking with him in this way?
Miki: I do love talking with him. It is fun.

When Miki was talking with Tom, Yuri (I) was in a group just behind Miki's group. Showing the same scene that Miki had watched, Yuri responded in the following way.

Interviewer: What do you think of this scene (where Miki was talking with Tom)?
Yuri: Seeing Miki and Tom? … Well, nothing.
Interviewer: Have you ever asked Tom for help in the classroom?
Yuri: I think I have asked him a few times during this semester.
Interviewer: Do you like asking Tom to come and help you?
Yuri: No, I don't like that.
Interviewer: Then, do you like Tom himself coming to your group?
Yuri: I feel tense.

Notice the stark contrast in asking for help from the instructor between Miki (E) and Yuri (I). While Miki appears to like talking with Tom individually, Yuri reported feeling tense in conversation with Tom, and consequently Yuri preferred to refrain from asking for help from him. Interestingly, Miki did not always consciously use the strategy of asking for help as was shown in the stimulated recall interview.

4.3.2. Supplemental interviews

Immediately after the stimulated recall interviews, general interviews about participants' background and learning history were conducted. The interviews were individually conducted separately from the stimulated recall interviews, although the results are shown together here. The interview was conducted in Japanese and later the transcript was translated into English.

Miki and Yuri were both second-year college students, 19 years of age, majoring in English at a well-known and accredited Japanese women's university, They shared the same kind of background in that they started learning English at the age of 13 as part of formal English education in Japanese junior high schools, and then continued to study English at Japanese public high schools. Neither had any experience of studying abroad or staying in other countries for more than two weeks. Their general motivation for learning English was assumed to be higher than general university students in Japan. That can be inferred from their responses; when asked why they majored in English, they said that they would like to develop their English ability so that they could communicate with people around the world in English.

Being asked what kinds of English courses they have taken since entering the college, Miki and Yuri responded in the same way. In their first year, they took six English-skill focused courses in total as required: one listening (LL class), one writing, two reading courses taught by Japanese teachers, and two courses taught by native English speakers, in which Miki and Yuri reported that they had opportunities to participate in many communicative activities. In addition, they took content-based introductory English courses such as English literature, culture, linguistics, and communication. These were all required courses for first-year students, and Miki (E) and Yuri (I) reported that they could not choose other elective English courses because their schedules were too full.

Interviewer: How did you like your first-year English courses? Did you find any difference from your high school English classes?

Miki: I liked all the English skills courses, but especially I liked the oral English courses. In my high school days, I had an oral English course once a week (50-minute unit) only when I was in the first year. The rest of the English courses emphasized reading skills and grammar for preparing for entrance exams of universities. So, by taking oral English courses in this college, I felt that I am learning real English, and I was happy.

Yuri: Among the four skills courses, I liked the listening course (LL) the best. I liked the task of doing dictations of the movie, "Father of the Bride". I spent much time every week for the assignment to listen to the tape of the movie and do a dictation. Especially it was fun when I understood what was said.

Miki, when asked about the listening course (LL), responded that she attended regularly and she felt that the course was easy because she was not asked to say anything in class. She sometimes felt that the weekly assignment of dictations of the tape was tedious. As for the oral English class, Yuri responded that she did not like her first-year oral English teacher because he was so strict, but she liked the second-year teacher Tom. Yuri felt nervous about speaking English because she thought that she could not express herself perfectly.

The two students were also asked about the frequently and infrequently used strategies. In regard to the use of an electronic dictionary, both Miki and Yuri have been using it since their high school days, and bring it to all English classes. They both have bilingual printed English dictionaries, but they seldom use them because they are heavy and not easy to use. As for one of the infrequently used strategies – to talk to native English speakers outside the classroom – they responded as follows:

Interviewer: You can find many native English speakers like Tom in this college. Do you visit their offices to ask questions or to talk with them?

Miki: I have never done this.

Interviewer: Why not?

Miki: I do not know why, but I am just reluctant to do so.

Interviewer: Do you attend the out-of-class events such as welcome parties for international students from the U.S. or free chats with native English speakers?

Miki: Somehow I am reluctant to attend. I am very busy. I come to college almost every day, and I am busy for assignments and my part-time job at the convenience store.

Yuri responded in the same way: She does not work part-time, but she feels tired after the classes, and is busy with her assignments. As for the strategy of thinking in English, both Miki and Yuri responded that they had never thought of doing that. When asked about the future possibility of the use of this strategy, they both responded that it was impossible for them because they could not live without hearing Japanese in their daily life.

The supplementary interviews revealed interesting information about the students' backgrounds and their use of LSs. While both Miki and Yuri took the same courses in their first-year, their feelings about them were different: Miki enjoyed her English courses that native English teachers taught, and Yuri preferred the listening course (LL) that Japanese teachers taught in Japanese in the LL. About the use of LSs, both of them frequently used electronic dictionaries, but did not attend events held in English or talk with native English speakers outside the class even when it is possible to do so.

4.3.3. Summary

In the teacher-fronted situation (TF), both Miki (E) and Yuri (I) refrained from asking the instructor (Tom) questions to clarify his story or his directions for the assignment even when they needed to do so. In teacher-student interactions (T-S) in small groups, while Yuri remained reserved in interacting with Tom, Miki used the strategies of asking for help or clarifying the task. As a result she was successful in eliciting further related input from Tom. In the student-student interaction (S-S) in small groups, students did not use strategies in English. Instead, they overcame the difficulties in their native Japanese. The individual interviews revealed that Miki and Yuri had different preferences for courses offered in college, and that they were reluctant to attend the out-of-class activities held in English.

4.4. Phase III: LSs in an individual learning situation

4.4.1. Strategies used in Task A

Tasks A and B were designed to observe two ways of obtaining input; in Task A, participants get input from a non-human device, a tape recorder, and in Task B, from a native English speaker. The purpose of implementing these two tasks was to observe the similarities and differences of the use of LSs in relation to obtaining input from Es and

Is. As explained in Chapter 3 (see Table 5), Miki was the most extroverted, and Yuri was the most introverted student in the observed
classes.

The behavior of the participants was carefully observed paying
attention to how they obtained input from the tape recorder for the
designated five minutes. As a result, three types of strategies were
observed: taking notes, pausing the tape, and rewinding the tape to
listen again. Table 17 shows the use of those strategies by the two
participants. Task A was done individually.

Sequence of tape listening	Rewinding the tape		Pause		Taking notes	
	Miki (E)	Yuri (I)	Miki (E)	Yuri (I)	Miki (E)	Yuri (I)
1st time	0	0	0	0	0	(1)*
2nd time	1	3	0	3	0	4
3rd time	2	2	0	3	2	2
4th time	1	NA	0	NA	1	NA
Total	4	5	0	6	3	6 (1)

Table 17. Frequencies of strategies used in Task A. (* Parenthesis indicates that notes
were taken after the whole tape ended; NA: no 4th listening).

The first time, both participants listened to the tape from the beginning
to the end without stopping or rewinding the tape, which took about
one minute. Only Yuri took notes after listening to the whole tape.
From the second listening, Miki and Yuri stopped the tape to rewind.
In addition, Yuri paused the tape six times in total without rewinding
to think about what she had heard while Miki did not pause it at all.
Pausing the tape corresponded with taking notes; Yuri took twice as
many notes as Miki. Because Yuri spent more time in taking notes and
pausing the tape, she listened to the tape three times in total while
Miki listened to the tape four times.

It was noted that while Yuri was busy taking notes, looking at
the paper on which she was writing, except for operating the tape
recorder, Miki gazed at the tape recorder almost constantly. Although
this might not have been relevant in discussing the use of strategies, it
was interesting to observe the difference in the focus of their eyes.

4.4.2. Stimulated recall on Task A

Immediately after completing the task, a stimulated recall interview was conducted with the same participants; while watching the recorded videotape, the participants were asked what they were thinking when they were listening to the tape or they used strategies. The interviews were conducted individually in Japanese, and the results of the interviews synthesized so that the difference between the two participants could be clearly discerned. The detailed procedure of the stimulated recall interview was provided in Chapter 3.

The first question was about the first listening; both Miki and Yuri listened without stopping for the first time.

Interviewer: Why didn't you stop the tape the first time you listened to it?
Yuri (I):   This is my learning habit, and I am used to listening to the tape from the beginning to the end when I listen to the tape.
Interviewer: Then, what were you thinking while listening to the tape?
Yuri (I):   I tried to pick up as many words as possible.

Yuri followed her usual custom of listening to the tape from the beginning to the end without stopping it the first time. On the other hand, for Miki, estimating the length of the tape was her concern.

Miki (E):   I wanted to know how long this tape was.

Different reactions were observed after the first listening. Yuri wrote down words such as "wonderful woman" or "movies," while Miki did not take notes at all after her first listening.

Interviewer: You did not write down anything the first time you listened to the tape. Why not?
Miki (E):   I could not catch the outline of the story at all. Everything was blurred. I just knew that this story was something about "a wonderful woman".

Miki could have written down some of the words she understood if she had wanted to, but for her, grasping the overall meaning was more important, whereas Yuri wanted to focus on specific parts such as words or phrases.

With respect to rewinding the tape, Miki and Yuri revealed the same kind of intentions.

Interviewer: Why did you stop and rewind the tape here? This was different from your previous action.

Yuri (I): Because I could not pick up anything the previous time, I wanted to find any words or phrases I could pick up.

Miki (E): The second time I listened, I was able to increase my concentration. The first time I listened to the tape, I had something I was curious about, though I did not know exactly what. I stopped and rewound the tape in the place where I thought it was.

Yuri and Miki stopped and rewound the tape in places where they thought they could understand something. In other words, they were searching for understandable parts, and when it came to those parts, they would stop and listen carefully by rewinding the tape.

As to pausing the tape (this means pausing without stopping the tape), Yuri and Miki behaved differently. In terms of frequency, Yuri paused quite regularly and Miki did not pause the tape at all.

Interviewer: From here, you frequently paused the tape. Why did you do that?

Yuri (I): Here I thought I understood the story more than at other parts. I could not write notes without pausing the tape.

Interviewer: You continued to listen to the story without pausing....

Miki (E): Here, I wanted to grasp the holistic meaning of this story. If I constantly pause the tape, I cannot understand the big map of this story because the story is coming to me in segments.

The interesting thing was that Yuri took notes by pausing the tape and concentrating on writing notes, thus cutting off audible input from the tape recorder. Miki took notes without stopping the tape; listening while writing something was not difficult for Miki, but was a problem for Yuri. This was a noticeable difference between Miki and Yuri.

The stimulated recall with Yuri and Miki uncovered other interesting facts. For example, pausing and rewinding had several meanings for Yuri. Asked why she rewound the tape often, she said:

Yuri (I): I thought I could understand something when I paused the tape frequently.

> Yuri (I): I knew this part was telling about the place where they met. I knew it was some ladies' room, but did not know which ladies' room.
>
> Interviewer: In these cases, how did you solve this problem?
>
> Yuri: I tried to figure out by recalling the sound in my head.

For Yuri, creating silence by pausing and rewinding the tape was needed to recall what she had listened to in addition to writing down selected words. For Miki, however, taking notes after listening was more comfortable. After the second time she listened to the tape, Miki wrote down quite a few parts of her summary.

> Interviewer: Did you write down all of these after the second time you listened to the tape?
>
> Miki (E): Yes, I wrote about half of my summary all together. Something like, "she went for camping with wonderful woman". I also wrote "she met for the first time when she was waiting in line". But I did not know why she was waiting in line. I also wrote that "she wanted to travel, or liked to travel".

As for rewinding the tape, Miki had a different approach. Asked why she rewound the tape, she replied as follows:

> Miki (E): The tape says that she was waiting in line, but I wanted to know why she was actually waiting in line.

Miki was purposeful in listening. When she rewound the tape, she tried to search for specific information about the story. When she rewound the tape the fourth time she listened to it, she wanted to know whether the woman wanted to travel or she liked travelling.

4.4.3. Strategies used in Task B

The purpose of Task B was to observe how participants would elicit input by interacting with a native speaker of English (Karen: pseudonym). While implementing the task, I observed participants' behavior, paying attention to how they obtained input from Karen for the designated five minutes. Karen was an experienced English teacher who had been teaching English in Japan for more than 20 years. The interviews were conducted individually, and I synthesized the results of the interview so that I could see the difference between the two participants. I followed the same procedure as in Task A; the detailed procedure of the stimulated recall interview was provided in Section 3.4.2.

As a result of the observation, I found four types of strategies employed by the participants: asking to repeat the whole story, asking questions about the story to clarify or verify, requests to slow down, and note-taking.

Sequence of listening to the story	Request for repetition		Clarification or verification request		Request for slowing down		Taking notes	
	Miki (E)	Yuri (I)	Miki (E)	Yuri (I)	Miki (E)	Yuri (I)	Miki (E)	Yuri (I)
1st time	(1)*	(1)*	0	0	0	0	0	1(1)**
2nd time	0	(1)*	0	0	1	0	0	2(1)**
3rd time	(1)*	(1)*	4	0	1	0	(3)**	1(1)**
4th time	0	(1)*	0	0	0	0	1	1(1)**
5th time	NA	0	NA	0	NA	0	NA	0
Total	(2)*	(4)*	4	0	2	0	1(3)**	5(4)**

Table 18. Frequencies of strategies used in Task B. (*Parentheses indicate that the request was to repeat the whole story from the beginning; **Parentheses indicate that a memo was taken after the whole story ended; NA: no 5th listening).

In Task B, Yuri listened to the story five times, whereas Miki listened only four. As seen in Table 18, a large difference in the use of strategies between the two participants was also observed. Yuri (I) used repetition request strategies four times to elicit more input from the interlocutor. The participants needed to ask for the story to be repeated because Karen was told that she should not do anything without a request from the participants. Yuri also took notes more often than Miki (E) did. Throughout this task, Yuri spoke out four times in all, only when she requested to have the story repeated saying "Once more please". She did not make any other requests such as to slow down the rate of speech or to ask questions about the content of the story.

In contrast, Miki used various strategies: making requests or asking questions to make the input more comprehensible to her. For example, because the speech was designed to be delivered at the same speed as Task A – about 200 words per minute – Miki asked Karen to slow down, saying "Please speak more slowly". Furthermore, she spent quite some time to clarify the content of the spoken text itself in the third time she listened to the interlocutor as shown in Table 19.

Miki	Karen	Strategies
"Where did John meet Erika?"	"He met her at the job."	Clarification request
"Job?"	"Yeah."	Verification request
"What kind of job?"	"I don't know."	Clarification request
"What does, uh, did you mean 'clicked'?"	"Clicked means, uh, sometimes when you meet people, right away you like that person very much. In that case, we say, clicked." Karen explained with gestures, especially showing clicked by making sounds with her fingers.	Clarification request
"Please more slowly."	"Sometimes when you meet somebody and like that person right away. Somehow you like each other very much from the beginning,. In that case, in English we say 'clicked', 'they clicked', 'clicked'." This time Karen speaks more slowly with rather big gestures (exaggerated), repeating the same gestures twice.	Request to slow down
"Okay."		

Table 19. Interaction between Miki and her interlocutor.

Miki asked about where John met Erika, or what the word 'clicked' meant. With regard to the particular meaning of the term 'clicked', it seems natural that the participants would have a question about the meaning of that because that term is not usually used in everyday life even though the word itself is familiar to university students because of its frequent use on the Internet. In addition, the interlocutor used a gesture, snapping her fingers when she read it. One interesting contrast is that Yuri did not observe the interlocutor's gestures because her focus was on her paper as described below.

Differences were observed in the two students' attitudes while listening to the interlocutor's talk. Although Miki (E) was watching the interlocutor carefully, specifically the movement of her mouth while listening to her English, Yuri (I) took quite a different approach to listening. Yuri never made eye contact with the interlocutor except when requesting the interlocutor to repeat. She even looked as if she was intentionally turning her eyes away from the interlocutor. Also a difference in their attitudes to taking notes was found. Yuri (I) spent more time writing down key words, and possibly significant words or phrases, while Miki (E) wrote less. The reason might be that Miki was actually busy watching the interlocutor's mouth movements, asking questions and making sense of the story she heard.

4.4.4. Stimulated recall for Task B

In the stimulated recall interviews, an attempt was made to elicit information about what the two participants were thinking while listening, especially when they needed to clarify the interlocutor's talk. Although the same interview procedure was used for both participants, the amount of information retrieved from them was quite different: in general, Miki (E) spoke more fluently, and Yuri (I) spoke less. Miki, who used more socio-affective strategies than Yuri, had more things to talk about.

In the observation it was found that Miki carefully looked at the interlocutor while Yuri did not look at Karen except for a few occasions. With regard to this point, Miki said the following:

Interviewer: What were you thinking then?

Miki: I was thinking about what she said by watching her mouth movements.

Interviewer: Why did you watch her mouth?

Miki: Somehow, I can understand what she is trying to say by watching her mouth movements. Of course, it is not perfect, but it is much better than not watching them.

On the other hand, Yuri responds like this.

Interviewer: What were you thinking then?

Yuri: I think I was giving a blank look. I wasn't thinking anything.

Although this behavior of looking at the source of input did not necessarily aid Miki in processing the tape input in Task A, it worked as a conscious and beneficial strategy in Task B.

While Miki used clarification requests such as asking the content of the story, Yuri did not use any communication strategies. This does not necessarily mean that Yuri did not feel the story was easy or got easier by listening to it many times.

Interviewer: Then, this is the third time to listen, and did you understand better than before this time?

Yuri (I): I did not feel any changes (in my understanding).

The question here is why Yuri did not ask any questions about the story instead of simply asking to repeat the whole story. In contrast, Miki asked questions freely.

Interviewer: What were you thinking then (at the point where Miki asked about where they met)?

Miki (E): I caught the word 'train' so I thought they met on the train. I wanted to check that out, but I found out it was wrong, contrary to my first thought.

While listening, Miki was hypothesizing about the story with several key words she heard. In addition to 'train', with the word 'movies' she also hypothesized that it might be related to the job of the author.

Miki (E): I was wondering what "movies staff (this was mishearing; actually Karen said "movies and stuff") meant. I thought the movie was related to her job. Therefore, I asked what her job was.

Although she did not correctly comprehend the story, she was actively thinking about the story and asked Karen to confirm whether or not her hypotheses were right. By asking questions, Miki modified the input to adjust to her proficiency level. In this point, she differed from Yuri. With regard to asking questions, however, even Miki was not totally uninhibited. Miki thought that Karen's way of speaking was rather fast and she wanted her to slow down, but she needed some time to express this request.

Interviewer: What were you thinking while listening to the story for the second time?
Miki (E): I had made up my mind to ask her to slow down.

Of course, she could have asked her to slow down in the middle of listening to the story, but she chose to wait until the story ended. This was also true of the previous "movies and stuff". The source of misunderstanding was that she did not know the use of the word "stuff" and from the similar pronunciation, she misunderstood that it was "staff" instead of "stuff". Although she did not agree with the response by Karen, Miki hesitated to question further. As the proof of that, she revealed that she did not know what the phrase "movies and stuff" meant after all.

Interviewer: After finishing the task, did you have anything to say?
Miki (E): With the key word "movies staff," I asked about Erika's job. But the response was that there was no information about her job. I still wonder what "movies staff" meant. Was it "moving" staff instead of "movies?"

This might be because she did not know how to elaborate the question in English.

She asked the interlocutor to slow down when she asked about the meaning of 'clicked' by saying "Please more slowly".

100

Interviewer: You looked embarrassed. What made you look like that?

Miki (E): I thought I did not understand exactly what she meant, though I tried to guess what she meant.

4.4.5. Summary of Phase III

The Phase III study pointed to the fact that in listening to the tape (Task A), Yuri (I) used more strategies than Miki (E). Yuri rewound the tape more often and took more pauses while listening to the tape. Miki listened to the whole story and just rewound to listen to the whole story again. On the other hand, in listening to a story from a native English speaker (Karen), Miki used more strategies in eliciting further information from Karen than Yuri did. Miki used a variety of strategies to make Karen's story more comprehensible to her. While Yuri just made a request to Karen to repeat the whole story, Miki asked questions to clarify the story, and made a request to slow down the speech. In Task B, the focus of concentration also differed. While Miki made eye contact with Karen, Yuri did not appear to look at her. Also in Task A, while Miki looked at the tape recorder from which the story came, Yuri focused on her paper.

5. Discussion

5.1. Introduction

This chapter presents the answers to my three research questions, based on the results of Phases I through III.

5.2. Responding to Research Question 1

My first research question addresses the following: 'What are the characteristic strategies of Japanese college students in the EFL context?'

5.2.1. Discussion of the difference between present strategy use and previous use

When comparing the 'use' of the four types (modes) of LSs, the mean of communication strategies was the highest, and that of cognitive strategies was the lowest (Table 10, Figure 8). The present use of cognitive strategies was less than reported previous strategy use, but in contrast, the use of communication and socio-affective strategies increased with metacognitive strategies remaining almost the same. Yang (1996), who investigated the strategy use of EFL students in Taiwan university students, reported similar tendencies: participants used communication, affective and metacognitive strategies most.

Cognitive strategies are generally the most frequently used strategies with language learners (Oxford 1990), but the results of the present study seem to reflect a different pattern of use, probably based on the particular learning conditions of this sample. The use of LSs can change as learners pass through various stages of education from junior high school to university (Brown 2000, Takeuchi/Wakamoto 2001). Sharp disciplinary differences in strategy use by college majors have been reported (Oxford/Nyikos 1989, Peacock/Ho 2003). In addition, changes in LS use depending on the proficiency of the learners were found by Vandergrift (1997). Comparing novice and intermediate high school learners of French in Canada, he found that novice learners reported more use of cognitive strategies than intermediate learners. These changes differ from the strategies associated with learner factors such as personality types, as will be discussed in the next section.

Considering that the participants in this study were all college students majoring in English, it is possible that there was no longer the emphasis on cognitive strategies such as rote memory commonly used by high school students preparing for entrance exams, and that students had shifted their focus to strategies that could be used in real communication situations. Such strategies include communication strategies or socio-affective strategies that deal with the learners' affective domain or facilitate learning through interacting with other people. In fact, Figure 8 illustrates that learners reported using cognitive strategies rather often in the past. It is reasonable to assume that those who were studying for the entrance examinations used rote memory strategies, such as memorizing words by repetition, because entrance examinations have usually focused on reading comprehension, grammar, and vocabulary, and excluded speaking and listening.[15] Wakamoto's research on strategy use of junior high school students (1992), and strategy use of junior and senior high school students (1998), found that cognitive strategies useful for exams were most frequently used by all the participants, although successful language learners used additional cognitive strategies such as listening to TV or radio language programs, which was also reported by Huang and Van

---

15   As for listening, the National Center for University Entrance Examinations (NCUEE) started to include a listening test in the National Center Test for University Admissions in 2005. Details are shown in NCUEE (2006), but most private universities are reluctant to introduce a listening test because of administrative difficulties (Law 1994).

104

Naerssen (1987). Thus, the goals of and approach to learning appear to change as learners pass through the various educational levels.

Frequently used individual strategies also reflect such tendencies (see Table 11). Communication strategies such as guessing, using synonyms or gestures, and socio-affective strategies such as requesting to repeat or rewarding oneself were most common. The frequent use of these strategies indicates that learners were more engaged in communicative activities in their language learning than in their high school days. Indeed, both participants, Miki and Yuri, reported that they had opportunities to participate in many communicative activities in their first-year oral communication classes that English native speakers taught.

While the mean of metacognitive strategies was rather low compared to cognitive strategies, individual metacognitive strategies such as learning from their own mistakes, having long-term objectives or making self-evaluations were also found to be frequently used. This shows that there is some variation in the use of metacognitive strategies. As Wenden (1987b, 1998) states, metacognitive strategies are important to control one's own learning and especially significant for adult learners who need to learn independently because, unlike junior or high school students, they cannot rely on teachers all the time, and instead they need to plan their learning by setting their own goals, evaluating themselves, and modifying their plans. Students presently at university are under pressure to improve their practical English ability in order to find jobs after their graduation. The influence of English proficiency on job prospects may help to explain the presence of metacognitive strategies among the most frequently used LSs.

The only cognitive strategy that was listed in Table 11 was that of 'using references'. Classroom observation and individual interviews with Miki and Yuri revealed that the reference most often used is the ubiquitous electronic dictionary; learners inevitably encounter unknown vocabulary items in their studies and they need to overcome such difficulties. In this sense, it is quite natural to use references in their learning, except in the cases of taking exams or having conversations with other people.

The data on frequently used individual strategies seem to indicate that they were all rather easily applied: When time and circumstances allow, learners use electronic dictionaries, and make inferences when they cannot use dictionaries. The only exception is requesting to repeat, which inevitably needs other people with whom to talk and to ask questions. It is interesting that Japanese learners of English reported using this clarification request strategy despite the potential difficulty.

5.2.2. Discussion of the gap between use, preferences, helpfulness, and previous use

As the analysis of Phase I results indicated (Table 10, Figure 8), the perception of 'helpfulness' for the four types of LSs was highest among the four dimensions, and that of 'preference' was higher than the two other dimensions – present use and previous strategy use – of LSs. The gaps between 'perception of helpfulness' and those of 'use' and 'previous strategy use' were notably large. This indicates that although learners thought that using LSs was helpful for improving their English ability, or learners preferred to use LSs, they hesitated to employ them. Table 12 lists the ten least frequently used LSs of the Japanese female college students in this study. In this regard it is also useful to consider exactly why those strategies were less used. I argue that the influence of the EFL environment, the Japanese specific learning context and culture, lead to the infrequent use of such strategies.

For example, 'participating in out-of-class events' and 'thinking in English' were the least used strategies (Table 12). Out-of-class events give learners opportunities to expand their listening and speaking, and EFL learners should use this strategy because they are disadvantaged compared to ESL learners who have more chances to be exposed to English in their daily life. Brown (2005: 11) also suggests that in addition to attending college English courses, a substantial amount of out of class self-study is required to attain higher English ability in Japan. In reality, English learners need to use some resources to find those events such as searching through magazines or reading the bulletin board, and thus they might have to make special efforts to find appealing out-of-class-events because these occasions of out-of-class events themselves are rare and the types of events are limited.

106

However, it is also true that several English-speaking events were available to the participants, such as welcome parties for international students from the U.S, or weekly free English chat opportunities with English native speakers. Miki (E) revealed in her interview that she had never participated in such an activity because "somehow she was reluctant to attend". One reason could be that students were just not inclined to study hard. Brown (2005) suggests that Japanese college students do not have enough time to devote to English study without sacrificing their college life filled with heavy course loads in the daytime and part-time jobs in the evening.

Similarly, reasons for the less frequent use of 'thinking in English' seem to lie in the EFL environment. We may think that learners could utilize this strategy anywhere regardless of their learning conditions. However, when interviewed, Miki (E) and Yuri (I), responded that this was impossible for them because they could not live without hearing Japanese in their daily life. The college they attended offered a certain number of English courses taught in English, but those courses were limited to those taught by English native speakers as Japanese professors seldom taught English courses in English. In those learning conditions, learners have difficulty in shifting their language to English and thinking their thoughts in English. This finding is in line with Dörnyei's (2005: 218) argument that individual differences (ID) factors are not context-independent, but rather we need to conceptualize ID factors as interacting with the situational parameters, such as ESL/EFL learning contexts and language classrooms.

With respect to 'finding a conversational partner' ($M = 1.78$; $SD = 0.97$), one can conjecture that this may be difficult in an EFL environment. It is not impossible, but compared to the ESL environment, it is more difficult for Japanese learners of English to find English native speakers around them to act as conversational partners. Although they could practice with their Japanese friends, also non-native English speakers, it is rare for them to do so. Actually they seldom practice English with their friends outside the classroom. This is an interesting phenomenon. Japanese people are generally believed to prefer group-oriented behaviors as can be typically seen in travel by groups; however, when it comes to learning, Japanese learners show less frequent use of cooperative learning strategies. This can be interpreted in various ways. Sullivan (1996), who examined the classroom behaviors of Vietnamese students, for example, introduces a statement of a Vietnamese teacher about the difference between North American and Asian culture in the language class: Cooperative learning to foster working together and to learn from each other was developed as a way to counteract the competition that separates individuals in a U.S. classroom, but it is not necessary for Vietnamese students who share the same values and similar background (34). Although we need to be cautious about the stereotypical categorizations of the terms 'Asian' or 'North American', it is interesting to see that Japanese and Vietnamese students share the same tendencies.

The reasons for the infrequent use of the above three strategies (participating in out-of-class events, thinking in English, and finding a conversational partner) can be attributed to environmentally poor conditions; however, as Oxford (1996) and Griffiths (2003) claimed, culture can also influence the use of strategies, as seen in the rare use of 'physically acting out new words', or 'keeping a diary'. Unlike environmentally difficult strategies, these strategies could be used in any context. Miki (E) and Yuri (I) both responded to the idea of remembering words by physically acting them out by reporting that they had not even imagined using such a technique. Instead, memory strategies, repeatedly writing or reading words aloud, were frequently used among Japanese learners. This might be due to the fact that Japanese learners have been trained in elementary school to remember many Chinese characters by applying those rote memory strategies and may have lost opportunities to expand their repertoire of strategies. As to keeping a learning diary, although attempts have been made to have Japanese learners keep such a diary (e.g., Fujiwara 1996), other researchers have reported infrequent use of this strategy among Japanese learners (e.g., Takeuchi 1993). Research has not yet conclusively discovered why Japanese people tend to refrain from writing their thoughts about English learning in diaries.

In recent years, however, English-mediated instruction has become more prevalent from elementary school to university level. For example, MEXT selected about 100 high schools (Super English Language High Schools = SELHis) to teach general school subjects such as chemistry and world history in English in order to develop

108

Japanese students' communicative ability in English (MEXT 2003). With the expansion of English-mediated instruction, the strategy of 'thinking in English' will probably become more common.

A major factor affecting the infrequent use of a particular kind of strategy is the EFL context, which is not conducive to strategy use. Using strategies in this context may be seen as requiring a lot of effort. As for thinking in English, participating in out-of-class events, or finding conversational partners, for example, efforts are needed to use those strategies because the learning context does not provide learners with optimal conditions.

In the case of less frequently used strategies, intensive learning or spiral review, the EFL learning context does not seem to play as large a role. With spiral review, also called structured reviewing, learners keep spiraling back to what has been learned in carefully spaced intervals such as a day later, two days later, or a week later (Oxford 1990: 42). Students may need self-motivation to continue to use those strategies. Even when the importance of spiral review or intensive learning is recognized, it may be rather difficult psychologically for those who have already passed the entrance examination to employ those strategies to study English. The entrance examination system and educational credentialism have often been criticized as weaknesses of the Japanese educational system (Doyon 2001), and there is little doubt that university entrance examinations have a strong influence on the way foreign languages are taught and learned in Japan (Law 1994, Yoshida 2003). As mentioned in Murphey (2004: 704), "In-service and pre-service teachers liked my interactive classes and presentations, but most said they could not use these methods because they needed to train students to pass the entrance exams." In this sense university students need to reset their learning objectives and motivate themselves to study hard after entering the universities. Dörnyei (2005) argues that cognitive and metacognitive strategies are the most affected by motivation and social strategies are the least affected. Without strong motivation to improve one's own English proficiency, learner use of cognitive or metacognitive strategies might not increase.

Other factors affecting the choice of strategies, as suggested in Takeuchi (2003b), include the balance between the time needed to utilize a strategy and its effect, and the balance between cost and effect. That is, learners apply strategies only when they are convinced that it is worth using the strategy even though it requires spending some time or some money for private lessons. For example, 36.9% of elementary school pupils, and 50.9% of junior high school students attend *juku* (cram schools) after school (MEXT, 2005), and they spend much time and money at *juku* (Nishino/Larson 2003).[16] About 3000 private English conversation schools exist in Japan, which attract about 300,000 new students every year and about 700,000 people are learning English conversation skills (Ministry of Economy Trade and Industry 2006). These are good examples of cost effectiveness. Thus, Takeuchi's study offers invaluable insight into learners' strategy use; the need to motivate oneself to make an effort is also related to this kind of time or cost effectiveness.

The data on infrequently used individual strategies may thus reflect Japanese contextual or cultural characteristics.

5.3. Responding to Research Question 2

My second research question asks: 'What are the characteristic strategies of extroverts and introverts in the Japanese college context?'.

5.3.1. General tendencies from quantitative data

The results of Phase I identified the perceptions of LS use by extroverts and introverts. Examining the four modes of LSs, cognitive, metacognitive, communication, and socio-affective, differences were observed in one dimension (preference) of the metacognitive mode in

---

16   In addition to *juku*, Riley/Takai/Conaty (1998) present home tutors and correspondence course as the types of extra school forms of education, and describe them as a dense network or as 'shadow education' to shadow the curriculum offered in the public schools.

that Es showed significantly higher preferences for metacognitive strategies than did Is (see Table 14). According to Vandergrift (1997), the use of metacognitive strategies should have been key in making Es more successful listeners; however, in this study, Es showed a stronger preference for metacognitive strategies than did Is, but in their present or previous use of or awareness about helpfulness, no significant differences were found. Therefore the listening proficiency of Es was not found to be significantly higher than Is. This can be interpreted in various ways, but one possibility is that Es may want to use more metacognitive strategies, but some factors, environmental or cultural factors, for example, interfere with their intentions. This will be discussed further in a later section.

Differences were also noted in three dimensions of the socio-affective mode, i.e., preference, present strategy use, and previous strategy use (see Table 15). Is' preference for the socio-affective mode was significantly lower than that of Es. In regard to the other socio-affective strategies, Es reported that they had used previous strategy use, and are now using present strategies more frequently than had Is.

These results were interesting in that all the dimensions that showed a significant difference in use between Es and Is were ones in which Es had a significantly higher rate of use (see Tables 14 and 15), and that Is seemed hesitant to use. For example, Is perceived socio-affective strategies as being as helpful as Es did (E's $M = 3.84$), but in their learning of English, Is reported using those strategies less frequently in the past and at present. One reason for the difference in use that can be inferred from these results is that although Is thought socio-affective strategies were helpful for their English learning, they did not use them because they preferred not to use them.

The analysis of questionnaire data by modes did not yield any characteristic LSs of Is. With respect to individual LSs, however, some strategies were found to be frequently used by Is (Table 16): requesting to repeat (socio-affective), and strategies to utilize grammatical knowledge (cognitive). Is' use of grammatical knowledge is especially noteworthy. Two important characteristics of this strategy are that it can be used alone without involving other learners, and it can be assumed to be more suitable in reading or writing activities rather than listening or speaking activities because explicit grammatical knowledge is more applicable when sufficient time is allowed, as argued in Krashen's (1985) monitor model. In bottom-up processing, language comprehension passes through a number of consecutive stages; in top-down processing, various types of knowledge involved in understanding language can be used in a flexible order (Buck 2001: 2-3)

Comparing the characteristic use of strategies of Is and Es, Es seemed to use strategies such as praising oneself or nodding that could be used to aid real communication. Oxford and Nyikos (1989) reported that Is in general prefer to be involved more in reading activities rather than speaking or listening activities, especially listening to people in face-to-face interactions. The results of this study also revealed the same tendencies.

It is worth noting that Is reported using a clarification request strategy often, although in general, they showed less preference for and less frequent use of socio-affective strategies as a mode. This kind of strategy, asking questions or making requests, is a significant way to elicit more input and to comprehend what was said. This will be further discussed in relation to the observation data and stimulated recall interview results.

5.3.2. Learning in the classroom

5.3.2.1. Teacher-fronted (TF) situations

When we turn our attention to the classroom situation, the use of strategies changes. As we have seen in the results of Phase II, the frequency of socio-affective strategies employed by Es and Is was not high. Especially in a teacher-fronted (TF) situation, the use of socio-affective strategies dramatically decreased. Through the classroom observations, I found that Es did not use clarification or verification request strategies in this situation. It was surprising that students did not ask questions regarding the assignment that was given by their instructor even when they clearly had trouble understanding what they were asked to do in the homework assignment. The strategy they adopted was rather interesting: instead of asking their instructor directly, they asked each other in Japanese about the assignment. Thus, in the teacher-fronted class, there was no observable variation in Es' and Is' use of strategies. It is interesting to consider why students avoid using socio-affective strategies in this situation.

The stimulated recall interview results of Phase II revealed that there were two reasons: (1) the two students interviewed thought they could deal with the problem by asking their friends questions; and (2) they were afraid of asking the course instructor questions. Regarding the first reason, Miki (E) mentioned that she tended to solve this kind of problem with the help of other students. In this sense, she used LSs, but not in English; the same phenomena were observed in small group observation, that is, S-S (student-student) interaction. She avoided asking her teacher because she thought that other students had understood what she had not. She also stated that it had been her way of confirming instructions and general comprehension in the classroom for a long time. She did not remember specifically when she had started, but upon reflection she said that she thought she had acquired that habit in junior high school. She began avoiding asking teachers questions in school subjects, including English, especially in a teacher-fronted situation. As might be supposed, asking questions was also awkward for the introverts. Yuri (I) responded that she had seldom asked questions in the classroom.

Although it has been stated that Japanese people are stereotypically described as introverted and it is important to be careful not to overgeneralize, we need to introduce the ideas of extroverts and introverts as two distinct groups of people. As Hofstede (1997) showed in Figure 3, personality is both acquired and learned. Tendencies toward personality traits are inherited, and culture influences personality: culture mediates personality and human nature. The concept of extroversion and introversion can be considered in the same way. Extroverts and introverts have inherited neurological features from their parents and their personality characteristics have developed on an individual basis. At the same time, they learn their own culture explicitly or implicitly, especially the type of classroom culture that teaches students to act as introverts. It is beyond the scope of this volume to describe and discuss Japanese personalities as a group or Japanese culture *per se*, but with regard to classroom culture, the Japanese have formed distinct social traits. It seems that they are trained to be silent in the classroom by teachers (Nozaki 1993). Unlike the case of North American classrooms, Japanese teachers try to control the class and keep students quiet when they think it is not an appropriate time for them to speak. In this sense, the discourse of silence rules (King 2005), and "The group dynamics among students and the active interaction between teachers and students so often seen in American classrooms seldom exist in Japanese classes" (Nozaki 1993: 28). It is natural for people to feel like talking when questions arise in their minds. Especially Es are supposed to have such an impulse because they are cerebrally underaroused (see Section 2.2.1).

There are good reasons why students are trained to be silent in Japanese classrooms. One is the large class size: as introduced in Chapter 2, Japanese classrooms are larger in class size compared to those in other developed countries like Canada, the U.K., or the U.S. (see Section 2.4.2). MEXT regulates that the class size can be up to 40 students in one classroom, although recent reform plans to reduce class size have been implemented at the prefectural level by hiring more teachers. The more students in a classroom, the less freedom students have, and the more discipline and rules teachers need to implement. Tani-Fukuchi (2005) argues from her study with Japanese university students that the larger classes and reduced opportunities to communicate with the teacher could contribute to higher levels of anxiety. Teachers also feel pressure teaching in a large class (Ryan 1995). With overcrowded classrooms, teachers cannot use a broad range of methods, and students are limited in the LSs they can use.

5.3.2.2. Student-centered (SC) situations: small group work

Evidence to support this comes from the classroom observations, where I noticed that when instruction was not so teacher-centered, the use of strategies gradually increased. Miki, an extrovert, called the instructor over to ask him questions about what she wanted to say and eventually elicited more stories (input) from him. In the stimulated recall interviews, when asked why she did not ask any questions in the teacher-fronted phase, Miki revealed that the climate in the whole class situation was not conducive to asking questions, and that she would feel awkward if she drew attention to herself. Even in the group or pair activity phase, Yuri, an introvert, revealed in the interview that she did not feel like asking questions or calling on the native speaker instructor for help. She simply preferred not to ask the instructor for help in the classroom, and it appeared that this was not influenced either by the size or atmosphere of the class; these remarks seem to have been prompted by her own personality trait. In this sense, Is probably do not suffer any frustration in learning in the Japanese educational context where learners are asked to keep silent and are not supposed to challenge teachers. On the other hand, for Es, this context does not seem to be appropriate. Although Es naturally prefer to use socio-affective strategies such as those of clarification or verification, they feel inhibited in Japanese classrooms. In conclusion, two factors mitigate against students' using socio-affective strategies: the large class size and the training they have received to keep silent. These are factors external to the learner, and should be distinguished from factors which are learner-internal (Nunan 1995).

In addition to the large class size, Japanese learners of English feel pressure from their peers. Greer (2000) suggests that Japanese learners of English are concerned about speaking English in contexts where other students speak in Japanese. As Miki revealed in the stimulated recall interview, students did not want to stand out in the group. An old Japanese saying warns: "The nail that sticks out is hammered down." Of course, this is not limited to learners and can be applied to Japanese people in general, and also to teachers as in the case of an anecdote introduced by Antepara (1995: 119): One older Japanese teacher once told me: "You have to do your job, but don't do it too well." The desire of Japanese to conform to a homogeneous society appears deeply ingrained (Harper 1995).

However, it does seem that learners feel considerable pressure in the classroom. When they ask questions in a whole group situation, they are afraid of being rejected by their peers for being conspicuous and in consequence, of being excluded from the group. This pressure encourages students to keep silent and refrain from asking the instructor questions for clarification or verification. On the other hand, Es are free from this pressure in small group or pair activities and are able to ask questions. It therefore seems possible to draw a reasonable conclusion that this pressure is real and consequently of considerable significance.

Regarding the second reason, Miki (E) stated that she was afraid of two possible problems. One of them was that she might be unable to express her questions properly in the target language. Unlike asking questions in Japanese, Miki needed to consciously compose her questions in English. Secondly, from her previous strategy use, she was worried about whether or not she could understand the response from the instructor. She stated that sometimes the course instructor responded to her in a way she could not understand, using difficult words she did not know.

Miki's first reason seems to reflect an important characteristic of Japanese learners of English. It would appear that Japanese students are socialized not to ask questions in the classroom.

5.3.3. Learning in an individual learning situation

The results of Phase III also supported the above tendencies. In the individual task with a native English tutor (NET) and a non-native learner of English, the extroverted student and the introverted student demonstrated a contrasting use of socio-affective strategies. Whereas Miki, the extrovert, employed various kinds of socio-affective strategies such as requests to slow down, clarification requests, and verification requests to receive fine-tuned input, Yuri, the introvert, did not use any of these strategies. Yuri just used the strategy of repeating her request to the NET to repeat the whole sentence again (Table 18). The task for the participants was to understand the NET's speech, and because the directions allowed them to ask any kind of questions or make any requests to the NET within the five-minute period, they could have done anything they wanted to. The conditions for both participants were identical. In analyzing their use of strategies, it is fairly certain that their use of strategies reflects their preferences for LSs and past learning habits. These results were similar to those obtained by Ehrman and Oxford (1990), in which extroverts preferred social strategies such as cooperation with others or asking for clarification, and introverts preferred to learn alone, and to avoid social contact (see Section 2.2.2).

The results of Phase I and III show that Es prefer to use interpersonal strategies (socio-affective) more than Is. As has been seen, what is interesting here is that both the Es and Is assume that socio-affective strategies are helpful for learning English (see Table 15). That is, for Is, although socio-affective strategies would seem helpful and effective, Is do not actually use those strategies compared to Es.

Summarizing the LS use by Es and Is, it can be said that Es have a natural preference for socio-affective strategy use. When offered the opportunity to use those strategies in more individual or small group interactions, Es attempt to employ socio-affective strategies, but they refrain from using those LSs in a teacher-fronted situation in class. Because Es have a natural preference to seek stimuli and excitement from outside (see Figure 2), they pose questions or try to increase opportunities for interaction with people. However, the present study suggests that Es have two problems in seeking stimuli from outside: the first lies in the class setting, and the second in Japanese classroom culture. Miki's (E) response to the question about why she did not ask questions in a teacher-fronted situation indicated that the classroom setting could be an inhibiting barrier for students for asking questions. In the classes observed, there were 22 class members, which was not an inappropriately large class for a language class by Japanese university standards. However, the classes in Miki's junior high or senior high schools were large with around 40 students in one classroom, so Miki stated that she had naturally formed the habit of not asking questions in a whole class situation. Although the college class size was small, it seems that students cannot change their classroom behavior easily. To discuss students' LS use, other factors such as differences of communication style between Japanese- and English-speaking societies, for example, classroom culture, turn-taking, and keeping eye-contact, need to be considered. However, from the perspective of E/I, an important difference in the socio-affective strategy of Es could be observed between the whole-class and individual learning situation. Therefore, it seems reasonable to assume that Es were socialized to behave like Is in the classroom by the Japanese educational system, despite their natural preferences.

Although Miki was questioned about how she felt about failing to ask questions in the whole class, she could not verbalize her feelings. It is probable that this means that the classroom culture she experienced during her school career is deeply rooted in her use of LSs at an unconscious level. As discussed in Chapter 2, personality is biologically inherited as well as learned through culture (see Figure 3). The data shown by the questionnaire (Phase I) indicate that more Es have the perception that they are using socio-affective strategies than Is do, but the result of classroom observation (Phase II) and individual task implementation (Phase III) demonstrates that their LS use changes depending on the kind of situation (Table 20).

	Natural preference	*In the class-room (whole)*	*In the class-room (group)*	*Individual interaction*
Extroverts	Frequent use	Infrequent	Rather frequent	Frequent
Introverts	Infrequent use	Infrequent	Infrequent	Infrequent

Table 20. Socio-affective strategy use in various learning situations.

5.4. Responding to Research Question 3

My third research question was as follows: 'Do extroversion and introversion have an impact on English proficiency as a foreign language, in particular on college learners' listening proficiency?'

The analysis of the results of the relationship between E/I and listening proficiency did not show any significant correlations between them. These results were similar to those of other studies: Busch (1982) found no significant relationship between E/I measured by EPI and English proficiency; Ehrman and Oxford (1995) found no significant relationship between E/I measured by MBTI and foreign language ability; and Carrell, Prince, and Astika (1996) found only a weak negative correlation between E/I and vocabulary test scores (see Section 2.2.2).

Nevertheless, the results of my study are interesting because it had been assumed that Es would improve their listening proficiency much faster and more efficiently than Is because they obtained more input from the instructor by employing socio-affective strategies more frequently. I suggest the following possible reasons for the lack of significant results in this study.

One possibility is that Is also receive the same amount of input by using different strategies. In the classroom, effective input eliciting strategies on the part of Is were not apparent. In the stimulated recall interview, however, Yuri (I) mentioned that she liked to listen to cassette tapes at home. As an assignment for another course she attended at her college, she was required to take dictation from a part of an English movie every week. Although Miki (E) was also given the same assignment, Yuri stated that she liked to stay in her room and repeatedly listen to the recorded English movies on her cassette tape; on the other hand, Miki mentioned that she did that assignment reluctantly. It was likely that Yuri spent more time than Miki doing that assignment, and as a result of that, although Yuri did not receive as much input as Miki in the classroom, Yuri compensated for this by listening to the tape at home. If this is true, Miki and Yuri may have received the same amount of input in total. This means that Es and Is use different LSs for eliciting input.

In addition, the learning context interacts with E/I in the achievement of listening proficiency. Japanese students are learning English in an EFL context, which is quite different from an ESL context in that students do not need to use English outside the classroom. Whereas Es receive more input in class as shown in the group-based activities (see Section 4.3.1.2), it is not easy for Es to find opportunities outside the classroom to talk in English with NSs (native speakers) or NNSs. If they were in an ESL setting, they would naturally make more use of the opportunities presented to them to interact in English with people (see Section 2.4.1), which would be good input to help improve their listening proficiency. In an EFL context, students can find listening resources on TV or the radio, and they can receive a certain amount of input through these media. The problem is whether or not Es can enhance aural input through non-human resources. In this sense, Is may have advantages over Es in an EFL context, which

119

is contrary to my earlier assumption. Thinking of Is' preference for learning alone through non-human resources, it seems evident that they may feel comfortable in increasing input through those media rather than with other speakers/individuals.

5.5. Summary

The impact of E/I on listening proficiency was not confirmed. In the end, instead of assuming a direct and linear link between personality traits and achievement, it might be more productive to postulate the impact of personality, extroversion and introversion, on the choice and use of LSs (Brown 2000, Dörnyei 2005). In this sense, the answer to the second research question about the choice of LSs by Es and Is becomes even more important. Although E/I did not have a direct and strong impact on the degree of an individual's listening proficiency, "they certainly shape the way people respond to their learning environment" and "people of different personality types pursue differential behavior patterns, which will have an impact on their participation in a range of learning tasks, from classroom activities to real-life practices of intercultural communication" (Dörnyei 2005: 30). Indeed, it is these patterns that enable researchers, teachers, and learners themselves to understand the learners (Ehrman 1996). In this regard, extroversion/introversion offers insight into individual differences among foreign language learners.

6.   Conclusion

The results of this study point to the following conclusions. In response to research question 1:
1.   Of the various types (modes) of strategies, Japanese college students use communication and socio-affective strategies most often, and cognitive strategies less frequently in their present situation compared to their previous use.
2.   Frequently and infrequently used strategies reflected the EFL learning context, learners' majors, Japanese culture, and their degree of comfort in using LSs.
In response to research question 2:
3.   Es perceive that they are using socio-affective strategies more frequently than Is do.
4.   In the teacher-fronted class phase, Es and Is did not use socio-affective strategies. This suggests that the traditional teaching methods in large classes may work advantageously for Is, who do not seek much in-class stimulation.
5.   In the group activities and individual learning situations, Es used socio-affective strategies more often than Is did.
6.   Is may prefer to listen to English using the tape recorder.
In response to research question 3:
7.   The impact of E/I on listening proficiency could not be confirmed.

The results of this study have important implications for pedagogy. In the group work in the classroom, Es and Is use socio-affective strategies differently. Teachers should be aware of these differences among learners and try to introduce various types of activities so that Es and Is can study appropriately and effectively. For Es and Is, creating an atmosphere in which both types feel safe to ask questions or have interactions with the course instructor is needed. This is especially true with Is, as Ehrman (1989: 179) suggests that "introverts would probably find it easier to make the most of the classroom experience if teaching staff were to help them understand that a classroom is a relatively safe place to practice language, a place where it is all right to try out new behavior and make mistakes".

In addition, teachers should be sensitive to the need to provide different kinds of assignments. Of course, in an EFL context, the opportunities to talk in English are limited (Krashen 1997), but teachers can give students assignments such as interviewing English speakers to encourage students to receive firsthand input from people.

6.1. Possible developments of this study

Finally, I will address the possible developments of this study: There are at least four.

In order to determine if learner strategy use associated with E/I would change depending on the situation, this study examined various situations. The questionnaire data (the SILL) of 148 students examined learner strategy use in general, whereas the case study of two students' strategy use while carrying out two tasks focused on individual learning situations. Classroom observation was especially important in identifying learner strategy use in an English class. I focused my attention on how learners used strategies to elicit more input from the instructor in a teacher-fronted situation and in group activity situations. Through the classroom observations and interviews, I found that learners hesitated to communicate in English. This kind of scene can be frequently seen in the language class as Aline (1995: 22) states: "as many teachers can probably verify, the task holds the students' attention for a limited time; soon they are speaking in Japanese with their friends." Especially when they had trouble in maintaining communication with other learners, they switched to Japanese and asked about or confirmed the information in their native language. In other words, in group activities students were using strategies in Japanese, not in English. Because my main emphasis was on strategy use in English, I therefore decided to focus on teacher-student (T-S) interactions rather than student-student (S-S) interactions. This did not completely eliminate small group data because some students used LSs with the teacher as representatives of their small groups. Moreover, L1 use is an important scaffold for L2 learning (Swain/Lapkin 2000). In future research, including LSs use in L1 should also be considered.

Further, this study includes possibilities of generalization. The qualitative data derived from Phases II and III contained rich and in-depth information in regard to the impact of E/I on learner strategies in practice and on English language comprehension. On the other hand, qualitative data are inappropriate to generalize because the number of participants is usually limited: this study focused on two participants in Phases II and III. Although this study adopted a three-phase design to avoid such limitations, we still must exercise caution about generalizing the results to other contexts.

Another limitation was that this study used only listening as a measure of proficiency. Because the main focus of this study was to observe the impact of E/I on how learners study English differently, it was legitimate to use listening as an evaluative tool. However, if another measure such as a test of oral proficiency had been used, we might have been able to observe another aspect of the influence of E/I.

Finally, to exclude gender influences on strategy use, I recruited only female participants for my study. It is clear that strategy use could vary in a co-educational situation where male and female students study together. For future study, it would be fruitful to include male and female participants to examine how strategy use would differ as a function of gender.

6.2. Pedagogical implications

I will address implications that can be derived from this study, both implications for Japanese learners of English and for English teachers in Japan.

My study revealed that extroverts and introverts had different preferences in the use of LSs, specifically in the use of socio- affective strategies. Introverts had a weak preference for socio- affective strategies, and tended not to use socio-affective strategies either in the classroom or in individual learning situations. However, strategy preference might be similar to the use of dominant and subdominant hands. People have a natural preference for the use of their hands and they use one hand more frequently and better than the other hand. However, people can still use the subdominant hand in their lives. Similarly, learners can be taught to use un-preferred strategies. Preference does not imply high or low ability. Every learner can develop their un-preferred strategies. In this sense, introverts can be taught to use their un-preferred strategies – socio-affective strategies as can be seen in Ehrman's (1996: 95) own reflection:

> as an introvert, I can gain great stimulation and pleasure from an academic conference at which I speak, meet new people, interact with old acquaintances, and so on. I have found, however, that to fully benefit from the conference, I have to find some time to read or work by myself. Only a few hours of 'introvert time' will do it, but if I do not get them, I lose perspective and behave in ways I regret later. Similarly, extroverts can study, write books, and enjoy time alone, but sooner or later they are likely to find themselves needing to seek some external stimulation, whether a conversation or just a dose of television news.

It is, therefore, fruitful for introverts to recognize that they can utilize socio-affective strategies in spite of their lack of preference for them. For that purpose, the first step should be for introverts to understand their own strategy use and preferences for strategies. Yuri, for example, did not explicitly recognize her strategy preferences or use of strategies. It is important to demonstrate to introverts that they are employing socio-affective strategies less frequently than Es and that it is because of their preference and not because of their ability.

Then, what implications are there for extroverts? The case of extroverts was rather complex because they seemed to be using strategies more frequently than Is. Extroverts had a strong preference for socio-affective strategies and used those strategies in individual learning situations. In this sense, they felt less stress and they were learning in accordance with their own preferences. The problem was in the classroom where they used socio-affective strategies less frequently in spite of their natural preferences. As Sakamoto and Naotsuka (1982) pointed out, Japanese people tend to play 'conversational bowling' instead of 'conversational volleyball or tennis'. Extroverts may feel a discrepancy between their natural preferences and the desired pattern of behavior in Japanese classrooms – in this case, reserved behaviors. Here, it is important to have extroverts recognize their strategy preferences and the reasons for the differentiated use of strategies in the classroom and in the individual learning situations. They should know that they could be encouraged to view their preferences positively and to use socio-affective strategies in the classroom.

In terms of pedagogy, the results of this study lead to two implications for teachers. The first implication is for classroom management. As I stated in Chapter 2, one of the characteristics of Japanese classrooms is the large class size. It is best suited for delivering information from teachers to students, but is not effective to facilitate interactions between teacher and students, or among students. This became obvious from this study. One of the reasons for the less frequent use of socio-affective strategies of extroverts can be assumed to be the large class size. As evidence of this, when the number of students involved in activities was reduced to small numbers, the use of socio-affective strategies increased. Although it is difficult to create contexts for individual learning in the classroom, teachers can make effective use of groups or pairs in the classroom. Interactions will most likely happen in group activities, and the use of strategies will be encouraged there.

However, teachers also need to remind themselves that students do not necessarily use English in group activities where teachers cannot completely control students. It is a dilemma for teachers. Instead of using strategies in English, students will easily switch to their native language, Japanese, to communicate when they talk with their peer students or to overcome communication problems. To avoid these situations, it is useful to show that speaking English among Japanese learners is effective in improving English proficiency. For that purpose, Japanese teachers of English need to show a 'model' that Japanese can use English in Japan. Ironically, because communication classes are usually taught by native speakers of English, Japanese learners rarely see Japanese people communicating in English in Japan. As Kouraogo (1993) argues, the difficulty in accomplishing the goal is "all the non-native speaker teachers who have not always mastered the language they teach" (167), and that not all the Japanese teachers of English are comfortable in speaking English in class. Besides, it is likely that they underestimate students' English abilities and often refuse to adopt communicative activities because they think that they are too difficult for their students (MacGregor 1995). However, seeing NNS teacher's role models will contribute to change the stereotypical image students have that English is just used for communicating with people from other countries.

The second pedagogical implication is the importance of recognizing the differences in strategy use associated with personality type. Teachers need to remind themselves that different types of learners are learning in the same classroom and that their use of strategies differs. This study implies that introverts might not employ socio-affective strategies even in group activities because they are reluctant to talk. To facilitate more strategy use by all learners including introverts, creating a risk-reduced learning atmosphere is needed. For example, encouraging students by providing positive feedback might be effective, and the demonstration of English use in the classroom or conducting English lessons in English might reduce the inhibition of learners because they do not have to switch from Japanese to English.

By focusing on the personality type of learners and associated learner strategies, I was able to identify how extroverts and introverts were using different LSs in a Japanese learning context. This should constitute a solid foundation for further research and I hope the implications derived from this study will contribute not only to helping Japanese learners to improve their English proficiency, but also to helping teachers in general to create an effective and appropriate curriculum for students in an EFL context.

References

Aline, D.P. 1995. Teaching in a Girl's Private High School. In Wada/ Cominos (eds), 20-26.

Anderson, J.R. 1983. *The Architecture of Cognition*. Cambridge, MA: Harvard University Press.

Anderson, J.R. 1995. *Cognitive Psychology and its Implications*. New York: Freeman.

Antepara, R.B. 1995. Speed Bumps: Mechanisms of Control in Japanese Schools. In Wada/Cominos (eds), 115-121.

Barbaranelli, C. / Capara, G.V. / Rabasca, A / Pastorelli, C. 2003. A Questionnaire for Measuring the Big Five in Late Childhood. *Personality and Individual Differences* 34, 645-664.

Bedell, D.A. / Oxford, R.L. 1996. Cross-cultural Comparisons of Language Learning Strategies in the People's Republic of China and Other Countries. In Oxford (ed.), 47-60.

Berry, V.E. 2004. *A Study of the Interaction between Individual Personality Differences and Oral Performance Test Facets*. Unpublished Ph.D dissertation. London: King's College, University of London.

Bialystok, E. 1985. The Compatibility of Teaching and Learning Strategies. *Applied Linguistics* 6/3, 254-262.

Bialystok, E. 1990. *Communication Strategies: A Psychological Analysis of Second-language Use*. Oxford: Basil Blackwell.

Bley-Vroman, R. 1989. What is the Logical Problem of Foreign Language Learning? In Gass, S. / Schachter, J. (eds), *Linguistic Perspectives on Second Language Acquisition*. Cambridge, UK: Cambridge University Press.

Brown, H.D. 2000. *Principles of Language Learning and Teaching*. New York: Longman.

Brown, J.D. / Robson, G. / Rosenkjar, P. 1996. Personality, Motivation, Anxiety, Strategies, and Language Proficiency of Japanese Students. *University of Hawaii Working Papers in ESL* 15/1, 33-72.

Brown, J.D. / Yamashita, S.O. 2000. English Language Entrance Examinations at Japanese Universities: 1993 and 1994. In Brown, J.D. / Yamashita, S.O. (eds) *Language Testing in Japan.* Tokyo: The Japan Association for Language Teaching, 86-100.

Brown, R.A. 2005. Autonomous Learning Strategies of Japanese EFL Students. *The Language Teacher* 29/4, 11-14.

Bruen, J. 2001. Strategies for Success: Profiling the Effective Learner of German. *Foreign Language Annals* 34/3, 218-225.

Buck, G. 2001. *Assessing Listening.* Cambridge, UK: Cambridge University Press.

Busch, D. 1982. Introversion-extroversion and the EFL Proficiency of Japanese Students. *Language Learning* 32, 109-132.

Carrell, P.L. / Prince, M.S. / Astika, G.G. 1996. Personality Types and Language Learning in an EFL Context. *Language Learning* 46/1, 75-99.

Cattell, H.B. 1989. *The 16 PF Personality in Depth.* Champaign, ILL:Institute for Personality and Ability Testing.

Chamot, A.U. 1987. The Learning Strategies of ESL Students. In Wenden/Rubin (eds), 71-83.

Chamot, A.U. 2001. The Role of Learning Strategies in Second Language Acquisition. In Michael, P.B. (ed.) *Learner Contributions to Language Learning: New Directions in Research.* Essex, UK: Pearson Educational Limited, 25-43.

Chamot, A.U. / Barnhardt, S. / El-Dinary, P.B. / Robbins, J. 1999. *The Learning Strategies Handbook.* New York: Addison Wesley Longman.

Chamot, A.U. / O'Malley, J.M. 1994. *The CALLA Handbook: Implementing the Cognitive Academic Language Learning Approach.* White Plains, NY: Addison Wesley Longman.

Chastain, K. 1975. Affective and Ability Factors in Second-language Acquisition. *Language Learning* 25/1, 153-161.

Chomsky, N. 1959. Review of B.F. Skinner's Verbal Behavior. *Language* 35, 26-58.

Cohen, A.D. 1987a. Studying Learning Strategies: How we Get the Information. In Wenden/Rubin (eds), 31-40.

Cohen, A.D. 1987b. Using Verbal Reports in Research on Language Learning. In Færch, C. / Kasper, G. (eds) *Introspection in Sec-*

ond Language Research. Clevedon, UK: Multilingual Matters, 82-95.

Cohen, A.D. 1994. Verbal Reports on Learning Strategies in Alternatives in TESOL Research: Descriptive, Interpretive, and Ideological Orientations. *TESOL Quarterly* 28/4, 678-682.

Cohen, A.D. 1998. *Strategies in Learning and Using a Second Language.* London, UK: Longman.

Cohen, A.D. / Weaver, S.J. / Li, T.-Y. 1996. *The Impact of Strategies-based Instruction on Speaking a Foreign Language.* CARLA Working Paper Series 4. Minneapolis, MINN: Center for Advanced Research on Language Acquisition.

Cook, V. 2002. Introduction to Chapter 9: Individual Differences in L2 Fluency: the Effect of Neurobiological Correlates, Jean-Marc Dewaele. In Cook, V. (ed.) *Portraits of the L2 User.* Tonawanda, NY: Multilingual Matters, 219-220.

Corder, S.P. 1967. The Significance of Learners' Errors. *International Review of Applied Linguistics* 5/2-3, 161-169.

Costa, P.T. / McCrae, R.R. 1992. Normal Personality Assessment in Clinical Practice: The NEO Personality Inventory. *Psychological Assessment* 4/1, 5-13.

Dadour, E.S. / Robbins, J. 1996. University-level Studies Using Strategy Instruction to Improve Speaking Ability in Egypt and Japan. In Oxford R. (ed.), 157-166.

Dewaele, J.-M. / Furnham, A. 1999. Extraversion: The Unloved Variable in Applied Linguistic Research. *Language Learning,* 49/3, 509-544.

Dörnyei, Z. 1995. On the Teachability of Communication Strategies. *TESOL Quarterly* 29/1, 55-84.

Dörnyei, Z. 2005. *The Psychology of the Language Learner.* Mahwah, NJ: Lawrence Erlbaum Associates.

Dörnyei, Z. / Scott, M.L. 1995. Communication Strategies in a Second Language: Definitions and Taxonomies. *Language Learning* 47/1, 173-210.

Dörnyei, Z. / Skehan, P. 2003. Individual Differences in Second Language Learning. In Doughty, C. / Long, M.H. (eds) *Handbook of Second Language Acquisition.* Malden, MA: Blackwell Publishing, 589-630.

Doughty, C. / Williams, J. 1998. Issues and Terminology. In Doughty, C. / Williams, J. (eds) *Focus on Form in Classroom Second Language Acquisition*. Cambridge, UK: Cambridge University Press, 1-11.

Doyon, P. 2001. A Review of Higher Education Reform in Modern Japan. *Higher Education* 41, 443-470.

Dulay, H.C. / Burt, M.K. 1973. Should we Teach Children Syntax? *Language Learning* 23/2, 245-258.

Dulay, H.C. / Burt, M.K. 1974. Natural Sequences in Child Second Language Acquisition. *Language Learning* 24/1, 37-53.

Ehrman, M.E. 1989. *Ants and Grasshoppers, Badgers and Butterflies: Qualitative and Quantitative Exploration of Adult Language Learning Styles and Strategies.* Unpublished Doctoral Thesis, The Union Institute Graduate School, Arlington, VA.

Ehrman, M.E. 1996. *Understanding Second Language Learning Difficulties.* Thousand Oaks: Sage Publishers.

Ehrman, M. / Oxford, R.L. 1990. Adult Language Learning Styles and Strategies in an Intensive Training Setting. *Modern Language Journal* 74/3, 311-327.

Ehrman, M.E. / Oxford, R.L. 1995. Cognition Plus: Correlates of Language Learning Success. *Modern Language Journal* 79/1, 67-89.

Ellis, G. / Sinclair, B. 1989. *Learning to Learn English.* Cambridge, UK: Cambridge University Press.

Ely, C.M. 1986. An Analysis of Discomfort, Risktaking, Sociability, and Motivation in the L2 Classroom. *Language Learning* 36/1, 1-25.

Eysenck, H.J. 1947/1998. *Dimensions of Personality.* London: Transaction Publishers.

Eysenck, H.J. / Eysenck, M.W. 1985. *Personality and Individual Differences.* New York: Plenum Press.

Eysenck, H.J. / Eysenck, S.B.G. 1968. *EITS Manual: Eysenck Personality Inventory.* San Diego: Educational and Industrial Testing Service.

Eysenck, H.J. / Eysenck, S.B.G. 1975. *EITS Manual: Eysenck Personality Questionnaire (Junior & Adult).* San Diego: Educational and Industrial Testing Service.

Fujiwara, B. 1996. Planning an Advanced Listening Comprehension Elective for Japanese College Students. In Graves, K. (ed.),

Teachers as Course Developers. Cambridge, UK: Cambridge University Press, 151-175.

Gardner, R.C. 2000. Correlation, Causation, Motivation, and Second Language Acquisition. *Canadian Psychology* 41/1, 10-24.

Gass, S.M. / Mackey, A. 2000. *Stimulated Recall Methodology in Second Language Research*. Mahwah, NJ: Lawrence Erlbaum Associates.

Gleitman, H. / Fridlund, A.H. / Reisberg, D. 1999. *Psychology*. New York: W.W. Norton & Company, Inc.

Gravetter, F.J. / Wallnau, L.B. 1999. *Essentials of Statistics for the Behavioral Sciences*. Pacific Grove: Brooks/Cole.

Green, J.M. / Oxford, R.L. 1995. A Closer Look at Learning Strategies, L2 Proficiency, and Gender. *TESOL Quarterly* 29/2, 261-297.

Greer, D.L. 2000. 'The eye of Hito': A Japanese Cultural Monitor of Behavior in the Communicative Language Classroom. *JALT Journal* 22/1, 183-195.

Griffiths, C. 2003. Patterns of Language Learning Strategy Use. *System* 31/3, 367-383.

Griffiths, R. 1991. Personality and Second-language Learning: Theory, Research and Practice. In Sadtono, E. (ed.) *Language Acquisition and the Second/foreign Language Classroom*. Singapore: SEAMEO Regional Language Center, 103-135.

Harper, G. 1995. Learning from our Students: Futoko. In Wada/Cominos (eds), 77-83.

Hassan, B.A. 2001. *Extroversion/Introversion and Gender in Relation to the English Pronunciation Accuracy of Arabic Speaking College Students (Technical Report)*. Mansoura, Egypt: College Of Education, Mansoura University (ERIC Document Reproduction Service No. ED454740).

Hofstede, G. 1997. *Culture and Organizations: Software of the Mind*. New York: McGraw-Hill.

Huang, L.-S. 2004. *A Little Bit Goes a Long Way: The Effects of Raising Awareness of Strategy Use on Advanced Adult Second Language Learners' Strategy Use and Oral Production*. Unpublished Ph.D dissertation, Ontario Institute for Studies in Education of the University of Toronto, Ontario, Canada.

Huang, X.-H. / Van Naerssen, M. 1987. Learning Strategies for Oral Communication. *Applied Linguistics* 8/3, 287-307.

JACET Education Research Group 2001. *Eigokakyoiku no kiso to jissen* [Foundations of teaching English]. Tokyo: Sanshusha.

Johnson, B. / Christensen, L. 2000. *Educational Research*. Boston: Allyn & Bacon.

Johnson, D.M. 1992. *Approaches to Research in Second Language Learning*. New York: Longman.

Jung, C.G. 1987. *Psychological Types* (M. Hayashi, Trans.). Tokyo: Misuzu Shobo.

Kagata, T. 1998. *Gakushusha no tsumazuki ni kansuru kenkyu: Chugakusei no bunkei, bunpo nitsuite no rikaido chosa oyobi eigogakushu ni kansuru anketo wo motoni* [A study of the relationship between English proficiency and learner strategies of Japanese junior high school students based on English grammar tests and the questionnaire on learner strategies]. Paper presented at the 10th annual conference of Japan Association for the Study of Teaching English, Tokyo, Japan.

Kern, R.G. 1989. Second Language Reading Strategy Instruction: Its Effects on Comprehension and Word Inference Ability. *Modern Language Journal* 73/2, 135-149.

King, J.E. 2005. The Discourse of Silence in the Japanese EFL Classroom. *The Language Teacher* 29/10, 11-14.

Kouraogo, P. 1993. Language Learning Strategies in Input-poor Environments. *System* 21/2, 165-173.

Krashen, S.D. 1982. *Principles and Practice in Second Language Acquisition*. Oxford: Pergamon.

Krashen, S.D. 1985. *The Input Hypothesis: Issues and Implications*. London: Longman.

Krashen, S.D. 1997. *Foreign Language Education: The Easy Way*. Culver City, CA: Language Education Associates.

Larsen-Freeman, D. / Long, M. 1991. *An Introduction to Second Language Acquisition Research*. New York: Longman.

Law, G. 1994. College Entrance Exams and Team Teaching in High School English Classrooms. In Wada, M. / Cominos, A. (eds) *Studies in Team Teaching*. Tokyo: Kenkyusha, 90-102.

Leonard, T.J. 1998. Japanese University Entrance Examinations: An Interview with Dr. J.D. Brown. *The Language Teacher* 22/3, 25-27.

Lightbown, P.M. / Spada, N. 1993, 1999, 2006. *How Languages are Learned*. Oxford, UK: Oxford University Press.

LoCastro, V. 1994. Learning Strategies and Learning Environments. *TESOL Quarterly* 28/2, 409-414.

Long, M.H. 1996. The Role of the Linguistic Environment in Second Language Acquisition. In Ritchie, W.C. / Bhatia, T.K. (eds) *Handbook of Second Language Acquisition*. New York: Academic Press, 413-468.

Macaro, E. 2006. Strategies for Language Learning and for Language Use: Revisiting the Theoretical Framework. *Modern Language Learning* 90/3, 320-337.

MacGregor, L. 1995. My Approach to Team Teaching. In Wada/ Cominos (eds), 42-45.

MacIntyre, P. / Noels, K.A. 1994. Retrospective Review Article: The Good Language Learner. *System* 22/2, 269-287.

McCrae, R.R. / Costa, P.T. 2003. *Personality in Adulthood: A five-factor Theory Perspective*. New York: Guilford Press.

McDonough, S.H. 1999a. Learner Strategies. *Language Teaching* 32, 1-18.

McDonough, S.H. 1999b. A Hierarchy of Strategies. In Cotterall, S. / Crabbe, D. (eds) *Learner Autonomy in Language Learning: Defining the Field and Effecting Change*. Frankfurt: Peter Lang, 51-60.

Ministry of Economy Trade and Industry 2006. *Tokuteiservicesangyo Dotaitokei Chosa* [Indices of Specific Service Activity]. <http://www.meti.go.jp/statistics/data/h2v1070j.html> [2006, August 21].

Ministry of Education, Culture, Sports and Technology 1989. *Course of Study*. Tokyo: Ministry of Education.

Ministry of Education, Culture, Sports and Technology. 1998. *Course of Study*. Tokyo: Ministry of Education.

Ministry of Education, Culture, Sports, Science, and Technology 2003. *Super English Language High School ni tsuite* [About Super English Language High Schools]. <http://www.mext.go.jp/b_menu/houdou/15/04/03040113.htm> [2004, May 5].

Ministry of Education, Culture, Sports, Science, and Technology 2005. *Gakkou chosa* [School Surveys]. <http://www.mext.go.jp/b_men u/toukei/001/05122201/001/001/002.htm> [2006, September 1].

Mitchell, R. / Myles, F. 1998. *Second Language Learning Theories*. London: Arnold.

Mulvey, B. 2001. The Role and Influence of Japan's University Entrance Exams: A Reassessment. *The Language Teacher* 25/7, 11-17.

Muranoi, H. / Chiba, M. / Hatanaka, T. 2002. *Jissennteki Eigoka kyouka kyoikuhou* [Practical English Teaching Methodologies]. Tokyo: Seibido.

Murphey, T. 2004. Participation, (Dis-)identification, and Japanese University Entrance Exams. *TESOL Quarterly* 38/4, 700-710.

Myers, I.B. 1998. *Introduction to Type*. Palo Alto, CA: Consulting Psychologists Press.

Myers, I.B. 2000. *Introduction to Type: Japanese Translation Version* (Y. Sonoda, Trans.). Tokyo: Kanekoshobo.

Myers, I.B. / McCaulley, M.H. / Quenk, N.L. / Hammer, A.L. 1998. *MBTI Manual*. Palo Alto, CA: Consulting Psychologists Press.

Myers, K.D. / Kirby, L.K. 1994. *Introduction to Type Dynamics and Development*. Palo Alto, CA: Consulting Psychologists Press.

Naiman, N. / Fröhlich, M. / Stern, H.H. / Todesco, A. 1978/1996. *The Good Language Learner*. Clevedon, UK: Multilingual Matters.

National Center for University Entrance Examinations 2006. *National Center Test for University Admissions for 2006.* <http://www. dnc.ac.jp/center_exam/listening.html>.

Nishino, H.J. / Larson, R. 2003. Japanese Adolescents' Free Time: Juku, bukatsu, and Government Efforts to Create More Meaningful Leisure. *New Directions for Child and Adolescent Development* 99, 23-35.

Nozaki, K.N. 1993. The Japanese Student and the Foreign Teacher. In Wadden, P. (ed.) *A Handbook for Teaching English at Japanese Colleges and Universities*. New York: Oxford University Press.

Nunan, D. 1995. Closing the Gap Between Learning and Instruction. *TESOL Quarterly* 29/1, 133-158.

O'Malley, J.M. / Chamot, A.U. 1990. *Learning Strategies in Second Language Acquisition*. New York: Cambridge University Press.

O'Malley, J.M. / Chamot, A.U. / Stewner-Manzanares, G.. / Küpper, L. / Russo, R.P. 1985a. Learning Strategies Used by Beginning and Intermediate ESL Students. *Language Learning,* 35/1, 21-46.

O'Malley, J.M. / Chamot, A.U. / Stewner-Manzanares, G.. / Russo, R.P. / Küpper, L. 1985b. Learning Strategy Applications of English as a Second Language. *TESOL Quarterly* 19, 557-584.

Oxford, R.L. 1986. *Development and Psychometric Testing of the Strategy Inventory for Language Learning (SILL).* Alexandria, VA: Training Research Laboratory, US Army Research Institute for Behavioral and Social Sciences.

Oxford, R.L. 1989. Use of Language Learning Strategies: A Synthesis of Studies with Implications for Strategy Training. *System* 17/2, 235-247.

Oxford, R.L. 1990. *Language Learning Strategies: What Every Teacher Should Know.* New York: Newbury House.

Oxford, R.L. (ed.) 1996. *Language Learning Strategies around the World: Cross-cultural Perspective.* Honolulu, HI: University of Hawaii Press.

Oxford, R.L. / Burry-Stock, J.A. 1995. Assessing the Use of Language Learning Strategies Worldwide with the ESL/EFL Version of the Strategy Inventory for Language Learning (SILL).*System* 23/1, 1-23.

Oxford, R.L. / Green, J.M. 1995. Comments on Virginia LoCastro's 'Learning Strategies and Learning Environments'. Making Sense of Learning Strategy Assessment: Toward a Higher Standard of Research Accuracy. *TESOL Quarterly* 29/1, 166-171.

Oxford, R.L. / Crookall, D. 1989. Research on Language Learning Strategies: Methods, Findings, and Instructional Issues. *Modern Language Journal* 73/4, 404-419.

Oxford, R.L. / Nyikos, M. / Ehrman, M. 1988. Vive la Différence? Reflections on Sex Differences in Use of Language Learning Strategies. *Foreign Language Annals* 21, 321-329.

Oxford, R.L. / Nyikos, M. 1989. Variables Affecting Choice of Language Learning Strategies by University Students. *Modern Language Journal* 73/3, 291-300.

Patkowski, M. 1980. The Sensitive Period for the Acquisition of Syntax in a Second Language. *Language Learning* 30/2, 449-472.

Paulauskas, S. 1994. *The Effects of Strategy Training on the Aural Comprehension of L2 Adult Learners at the High Beginning / Low Intermediate Proficiency level.* Unpublished Ph.D. thesis, University of Toronto.

Peacock, M. / Ho, M. 2003. Student Language Learning Strategies Across Eight Disciplines. *International Journal of Applied Linguistics* 13/2, 179-200.

Pinker, S. 1994. *The Language Instinct.* New York: Harper Pernnial.

Porte, G. 1988. Poor Language Learners and their Strategies for Dealing with New Vocabulary. *ELT Journal* 42/3, 167-172.

Quenk, N.L. / Hammer, A.L. / Majors, M.S. 2001. *MBTI Step II Manual: Exploring the Next Level of Type with the Myers- Briggs Type Indicator Form Q.* Palo Alto, CA: Consulting Psychologists Press.

Rees-Miller, J. 1993. A Critical Appraisal of Learner Training: Theoretical Bases and Teaching Implications. *TESOL Quarterly* 27/4, 679-689.

Reiss, M.A. 1985. The Good Language Learner: Another Look. *Canadian Modern Language Review* 41, 511-523.

Riley, R.W. / Takai, R.T. / Conaty, J.C. 1998. *The Educational System in Japan: Case Study Findings.* Washington, DC: National Institute on Student Achievement Curriculum and Assessment Office of Educational Research and Improvement U.S. Department of Education.

Robbins, J. 1996. *Language Learning Strategies Instruction in Asia: Cooperative Autonomy?* Paper presented at Bangkok, Thailand.

Robinson, P. 2002. *Individual Differences and Instructed Language Learning.* Amsterdam: Benjamin.

Rubin, J. 1975. What the 'Good Language Learner' Can Teach Us? *TESOL Quarterly* 9, 41-51.

Rubin, J. 1981. Study of Cognitive Processes in Second Language Learning. *Applied Linguistics* 11/2, 117-131.

Rubin, J. 1987. Learner Strategies: Theoretical Assumptions, Research History and Typology. In Wenden/Rubin (eds), 15-40.

Russell, T.M. / Karol, L.D. 1994. The 16PH Fifth Edition Administrator's Manual. Champaign, Ill.: Institute for Personality and Ability Testing.

Ryan, S.M. 1995. Understanding the Pressure on JTEs. In Wada/ Cominos (eds), 70-76.

Sakamoto, N. / Naotsuka, R. 1982. *Polite Fictions: Why Japanese and Americans Seem Rude to Each Other.* Tokyo: Kinseido.

Schmitt, N. / McCarthy, M. 1997. Editor's Comments – Acquisition Section. In Schmitt, N. / McCarthy, M. (eds), *Vocabulary: Description, Acquisition and Pedagogy.* Cambridge: Cambridge University Press, 228-236.

Schumann, J.H. 1979. The Acquisition of English Negation by Speakers of Spanish: A Review of the Literature. In Anderson, R.W. (ed.) *The Acquisition and Use of Spanish and English as First and Second Languages.* Washington, DC: TESOL, 3-32.

Skehan, P. 1989. *Individual Differences in Second Language Learning.* London: Edward Arnold.

Skehan, P. 1991. Individual Differences in Second Language Learning. *Studies in Second Language Acquisition* 13, 275-298.

Skehan, P. 1998. *A Cognitive Approach to Language Learning.* Oxford, UK: Oxford University Press.

Snow, C. / Hoefnagel-Höhle, M. 1978. The Critical Period for Language Acquisition: Evidence from Second Language Learning. *Child Development* 49/4, 1114-1128.

Sonoda, Y. 2000. *MBTI no Tebiki* [MBTI Manual]. Tokyo, Japan: Kanekoshobo.

Stern, H.H. 1975. What can we Learn from the Good Language Learner? *Canadian Modern Language Review* 31, 304-318.

Stern, H.H. 1983. *Fundamental Concepts of Language Teaching.* Oxford, UK: Oxford University Press.

Strong, M. 1983. Social Styles and Second Language Acquisition of Spanish-speaking Kindergarteners. *TESOL Quarterly* 17, 241-258.

Sullivan, P.N. 1996. Sociocultural Influences on Classroom Interactional Style. *TESOL Journal* 6/1, 32-34.

Susser, B. 1998a. EFL's Othering of Japan: Orientalism in English Language Teaching. *JALT Journal* 20/1, 49-82.

Susser, B. 1998b. The Author Responds. *JALT Journal* 20/2, 83-85.

Suzuki, J. 1998. *Ondoku no koka ni tsuite no jisshokenkyu* [An empirical study on the effect of reading aloud]. *LLA Kansai Chapter Research Bulletin* 7, 13-28.

Swain, M. 2000. The Output Hypothesis and Beyond: Mediating Acquisition through Collaborative Dialogue. In Lantolf, J.P. (ed.) *Sociocultural Theory and Second Language Learning.* Oxford, UK: Oxford University Press, 97-114.

Swain, M. / Burnaby, B. 1976. Personality Characteristics and Second Language Learning in Young Children: A Pilot Study. *Working Papers on Bilingualism* 11, 115-128.

Swain, M. / Lapkin, S. 2000. Task-based Second Language Learning: The Use of First Language Use. *Language Teaching Research* 4, 253-276.

Takanashi, N. 1999. Orakon G kakushin han he [To teachers teaching grammar in oral communication courses]. *Modern English Teaching* 35/12, 41.

Takanashi, N. / Takahashi, M. 1990. *Eigogakugairon: Atarashii jidai no Eigokyoujuhou* [Introduction to English teaching methodologies for the new century]. Tokyo: Kinseido.

Takashima, H. 1990. Televi rajio nadono hoso ya onseikyozai ha donoyouni riyou shitara yoika? [How do we make use of TV/radio programs and audio materials?] In Goshima, T. (ed.) *Q &A keishiki niyoru jido eigo kyoiku handbook* [Handbook on early English teaching by questions and answers]. Tokyo: Kyobundo, 111-114.

Takeuchi, O. 1993. Language Learning Strategies and their Relationship to Achievement in English as a Foreign Language. *Language Laboratory* 30, 17-34.

Takeuchi, O. / Tanaka, T. / Mishima, A. / Nakanishi, Y. / Fukuchi, M. 1998. *Gaikokugo gakushu houryakushitsumonshi (SILL) no datousei wo megutte* [A study on validity of the SILL]. Paper presented at the 24th annual conference of the Japan Society of English Language Education, Matsuyama, Japan.

Takeuchi, O. 2003a. What can we Learn from Good Foreign Language Learners? A Qualitative Study in the Japanese Foreign Language Context. *System* 31/3, 385-392.

Takeuchi, O. 2003b. *Yoriyoi gaikokugo gakushuhouhou wo motomete: gaikokugogakushu seikousha no kenkyu* [Seeking to find better foreign language learning strategies: Study of successful language learners]. Tokyo: Shohakusha.

Takeuchi, O. / Wakamoto, N. 2001. Language Learning Strategies Used by Japanese College Learners of English: A Synthesis of Four Empirical Studies. *Language Education and Technology* 38, 21-43.

Tani-Fukuchi, N. 2005. Japanese Learner Psychology and Assessment of Affect in Foreign Language Study. *The Language Teacher* 29/4, 3-9.

Tarone, E. 1980. Communication Strategies, Foreigner Talk, and Repair in Interlanguage. *Language Learning* 30, 417-431.

U.S. Department of Education 2000. *Digest of Education Statistics, 2000: Chapter 2. Elementary and Secondary Education.* <http://nces.ed.gov/pubs2001/digest/dt069.html> [2001, August 2].

Vandergrift, L. 1996. The Listening Comprehension Strategies of Core French High School Students. *The Canadian Modern Language Review* 52/2, 200-223.

Vandergrift, L. 1997. The Comprehension Strategies of Second Language (French) Listeners: A Descriptive Study. *Foreign Language Annals* 30/3, 387-409.

Vandergrift, L. 1998. Successful and Less Successful Listeners in French: What are the Strategy Differences? *The French Review* 71/3, 370-395.

Vann, R.J. / Abraham, R.G. 1990. Strategies of Unsuccessful Language Learners. *TESOL Quarterly* 24/2, 177-198.

Wada, M. / Cominos, A. (eds) 1995. *Japanese Schools: Reflections and Insights.* Kyoto: Shugakusha.

Wakamoto, N. 1992. *A Comparative Study of Differences in the Uses of Learning Strategies Between Effective and Less Effective Learners in an EFL Context.* Unpublished Mater's thesis, Hyogo University of Teacher Education, Hyogo, Japan.

Wakamoto, N. 1998. *Chukokosei no gakushu horyaku toha* [Learner strategies of Japanese junior and senior high school students]. Paper presented at the Japan Association for the Study of Teaching English, Kansai Chapter, Osaka, Japan.

Wakamoto, N. 2000. Language Learning Strategy and Personality Variables: Focusing on Extroversion and Introversion. *International Review of Applied Linguistics in Language Teaching* 38, 71-81.

Warschauer, M. 1996. Comparing Face-to-face and Electronic Discussion in the Second Language Classroom. *CALICO Journal* 12, 7-26.

Wenden, A. 1987a. Incorporating Learner Training in the Classroom. In Wenden/Rubin (eds), 159-168.

Wenden, A. 1987b. Conceptual Background and Utility. In Wenden/Rubin (eds), 3-13.

Wenden, A. 1991. *Learner Strategies for Learner Autonomy*. Hertfordshire, UK: Prentice-Hall.

Wenden, A. 1998. Metacognitve Knowledge and Language Learning. *Applied Linguistics* 19/4, 515-537.

Wenden, A. / Rubin, J. (eds) 1987. *Learner Strategies in Language Learning*. Englewood Cliffs, NJ: Prentice-Hall.

Wharton, G. 2000. Language Learning Strategy Use of Bilingual Foreign Language Learners in Singapore. *Language Learning* 50/2, 203-243.

White, J. / Ranta, L. 2000. *What you Know and What you Do: The Relationship Between Metalinguistic Performance and Oral Production in a Second Language*. Unpublished manuscript, Concordia University, Montreal.

Wilson, M.A. / Languis, M.L. 1990. Differences in Brain Electrical Activity Patterns Between Introverts and Extraverted Personality Indices and Types. *Journal of Psychological Type* 34, 14-23.

Wode, H. 1977. Four Early Stages in the Development of L1 Negation. *Journal of Child Language* 4/1, 87-102.

Yang, N.-D. 1996. Effective Awareness-raising in Language Learning Strategy Instruction. In R.L. Oxford (ed.) *Language Learning Strategies Around the World: Cross-cultural Perspectives*. Honolulu, HI: University of Hawaii Press, 205-210.

Yang, N.-D. 2003. Integrating Portfolios into Learning Strategy-based Instruction for EFL College Students. *International Review of Applied Linguistics in Language Teaching* 41, 293-317.

Yoshida, K. 2003. Language Education Policy in Japan: The Problem of Espoused Objectives versus Practice. *Modern Language Journal* 87/2, 290-292.

Appendices[17]

Appendix A: The modified SILL 0.3b, developed for the Pilot Study

Modified Strategy Inventory for Language Learning (SILL) Version 7.0. Originally developed by R. Oxford, 1989.[18]

* For the pilot study, the Japanese written questionnaire was used.

The strategy inventory for language learning (SILL) is designed to gather information about how you, as a student of a foreign language, go about learning that language. On the following pages, you will find statements related to learning a new language. Please read each statement. On the separate answer sheet, mark the response (1, 2, 3, 4, 5) that tells (1) how true the statement is in terms of what you actually do when you are learning the new language – USE; (2) how helpful the statement is for your learning English – HELPFULNESS; and (3) how you like the statement – your PREFERENCES.

1. Never or almost never true of me
2. Generally not true of me
3. Somewhat true of me
4. Generally true of me
5. Always or almost true of me

---

17   Every effort has been made to trace copyright holders and to obtain their permission for the use of copyright material. The author apologizes for any errors or omissions and would be grateful to be notified of any corrections that should be incorporated in future reprints or editions of this book.

18   The author wishes to thank Rebecca Oxford for granting him permission to reproduce the Modified Strategy Inventory for Language Learning (SILL) Version 7.0 on pages 141 and 145 (© R. L. Oxford 1989).

PART A

1. I use new English words in a sentence so I can remember them.
2. I connect the sounds of a new English word and an image or picture of the word to help me remember the word.
3. I remember a new English word by making a mental picture of a situation in which the word might be used.
4. I remember the word by drawing a picture.
5. I visualize the spelling of the new word in my mind.
6. I associate the new word with a familiar word.
7. I use rhymes to remember new English words.
8. I use flashcards to remember new English words.
9. I physically act out new English words.
10. I review English lessons often.
11. I remember new English words or phrases by remembering their location on the page, on the board, or on a street sign.
12. I place the new word in a group with other words that are similar in some way (for example, words related to clothing).
13. I list all the other words I know that are related to the new word and draw lines to show relationships.
14. I schedule my reviewing so that the review sessions are initially close together in time and gradually become more widely spread apart.

PART B

15. I say new English words several times.
16. I write new English words several times.
17. I imitate the way native speaker talk.
18. I memorize English sentences.
19. I read aloud English sentences.
20. I practice the sounds of English.
21. I use familiar words in different combinations to make new sentences.
22. I watch English language TV shows spoken in English or go to movies spoken in English.
23. I listen to the radio in English.
24. I read for pleasure in English.
25. I write notes, messages, and letters in English.
26. I write reports in English.
27. I write e-mail in English.
28. I read English web pages.
29. I first skim an English passage (read over the passage quickly), then go back and read carefully.

30. I look for words in my own language that are similar to new words in English.
31. I try to find patterns in English.
32. I find the meaning of an English word by dividing it into parts that I understand.
33. I try to understand what I have heard without translating it word-for-word into my language.
34. I try to understand what I have read without translating it word-for-word into my language.
35. I make summaries of information that I hear or read in English.
36. I use monolingual dictionaries to help me use English.
37. I use bilingual dictionaries to help me use English.
38. I look for similarities and contrasts between English and my own language.
39. I find the meaning of a word by dividing the word into parts which I understand.
40. I attend and practice in out-of-class events where English is spoken.

PART C

41. When I do not understand all the words I read, I guess the general meaning by using any clue I can find, for example, clues from the context or situation.
42. When I do not understand all the words I hear, I guess the general meaning by using any clue I can find, for example, clues from the context or situation.
43. If I am speaking and cannot think of the right expression, I use gestures.
44. If I am speaking and cannot think of the right expression, I switch back to my own language momentarily.
45. I ask the other person to tell me the right word if I cannot think of it in a conversation.
46. I will wait until the interlocutor guesses and suggests what I would like to say.
47. I make up new words if I don't know the right ones in English.
48. I read English without looking up every new word.
49. In a conversation I anticipate what the other person is going to say based on what has been said so far.
50. When I cannot think of the correct expressions to say, I find a different way to express the idea; for example, I use a synonym.
51. When I cannot think of the correct expressions to say, I find a different way to express the idea; for example, I describe the idea.
52. I direct the conversation to a topic for which I know the words.
53. I avoid topics for which I don't know the words.
54. I use, 'uh' (fillers) to fill pauses and to gain time to think.
55. I use hesitation devices such as 'Well', 'Now', 'Let's see', and 'As a matter of fact' to fill pauses and to gain time to think.
56. I will use all-purpose words: Extending a general, empty, lexical item (e.g., things, stuff, thingie) to contexts where specific words are lacking.

PART D

57. I actively look for people with whom I can speak the new language.
58. I try to notice my language errors and find out the reasons for them.
59. I learn from my mistakes in using English.
60. When someone is speaking English, I try to concentrate on what the person is saying and put unrelated topics out of my mind.
61. I try to find out all I can about how to be a better language learner by reading books or articles.
62. I try to find out all I can about how to be a better language learner by talking with others about how to learn.
63. I decide in advance to pay special attention to specific language aspects; for example, I focus on the way native speakers pronounce certain sounds.
64. I plan what I am going to accomplish in language learning each day or each week.
65. I arrange my schedule to study and practice English consistently, not just when there is the pressure of a test.
66. I arrange my physical environment to promote learning; for instance, I find a quiet, comfortable place to review.
67. I look for opportunities to read as much as possible in English.
68. I plan my goals for language learning; for instance, how proficient I want to become or how I might want to use the language in the long run.
69. I evaluate the general progress I have made in learning the language.
70. I take responsibility for finding opportunities to practice the new language.

PART E

71. I try to relax whenever I feel anxious about using the new language.
72. I make encouraging statements to myself so that I will continue to try hard and do my best in language learning.
73. I actively encourage myself to take risks in language learning, such as guessing meanings or trying to speak, even though I might make some mistakes.
74. I give myself a reward or treat when I do well in English.
75. I pay attention to physical signs of stress that might affect my language learning.
76. I keep a private diary or journal where I write my feelings about language learning.
77. I talk to someone I trust about my attitudes and feelings concerning the language learning process.

PART F

78. If I do not understand, I ask the speaker to slow down, using phrases such as 'Could you speak slowly?'.

79. If I do not understand, I ask the speaker to repeat, using phrases such as 'Sorry' or 'I beg your pardon'.
80. I ask other people to verify that I have understood or said something correctly using the phrase such as 'You mean ...'.
81. I ask English speakers to correct me when I talk.
82. I practice English with other students.
83. I have a regular language learning partner.
84. I have a language learning partner on the Internet such as an e-mail friend.
85. I ask for help from English speakers.
86. I ask questions in English classes.
87. In conversation with others in the new language, I ask questions in order to be as involved as possible and to show I am interested.
88. I try to learn about the culture of English speakers.
89. I pay close attention to the thoughts and feelings of the people with whom I interact in the new language.

Appendix B: The revised SILL1.0, developed for the final study (English translated version)

Revised Strategy Inventory for Language Learning (SILL), originally developed by R. Oxford, 1989.

* For the final study, the Japanese written questionnaire was used.

The strategy inventory for language learning (SILL) is designed to gather information about how you, as a student of a foreign language, go about learning that language. On the following pages, you will find statements related to learning a new language. Please read each statement. On the separate answer sheet, mark the response (1, 2, 3, 4, 5) that tells (1) how true the statement is in terms of what you actually do when you are learning the new language – USE; (2) how true the statement is in terms of when you studied English in the past – PREVIOUS USE; (3) how helpful the statement is for your learning English – HELPFULNESS; and (4) how you like the statement – your PREFERENCES.

1. Never or almost never true of me
2. Generally not true of me
3. Somewhat true of me
4. Generally true of me
5. Always or almost true of me

PART A

1. I use flashcards or similar devices to remember new English words or phrases.
2. I use vocabulary textbooks to remember new English words or phrases; for example, I use *Target* or *Word-finder for the TOEIC*.
3. I make a sentence with the new words or phrases, so I can remember them.
4. I write new English words or phrases several times to remember them.
5. I say new English words or phrases several times to remember them.
6. I use new English words or phrases in a real conversation to remember them.
7. I physically act out the new words.
8. I practice the sounds of English so that I can correctly pronounce them.
9. I watch movies in English.
10. I read aloud English sentences.
11. I try to talk like native English speakers.
12. I use familiar words in different combination to make new sentences.
13. I watch or listen to English language programs on TV or on the radio.
14. I read for pleasure in English.
15. I attend and participate in out-of-class events where English is spoken.
16. I take notes or write messages in English.
17. I use reference materials such as (electronic) dictionaries to help me use English.
18. I use the Internet to read, write, speak and listen to English.
19. I think in English in my daily life.
20. I look for patterns to help me use English.
21. I find the meaning of a word by dividing the word into parts which I understand; for example I understand 'unfriendly' by dividing it into 'un-friend-ly'.

PART B

22. If I am speaking and cannot think of the right expressions, I use gestures.
23. In a conversation or in a tape listening, I anticipate what is going to be told based on what has been said so far.
24. When I do not understand all the words I read or hear, I guess the general meaning by using any clue I can find, for example, clues from the context, situation or facial expressions.
25. When I cannot think of the correct expressions to say, I use synonyms.
26. When I cannot think of the correct expressions to say, I make up new words.
27. I ask the interlocutor to tell me the right word if I cannot think of it in a conversation.
28. I will wait until the interlocutor guesses and suggests what I would like to say.
29. I direct the conversation to a topic for which I know the vocabulary.
30. I use 'uh' to fill pauses and to gain time to think.
31. I avoid the topics that I do not know well.

32. I use hesitation devices such as 'Well', 'Now', 'Let's see', and 'As a matter of fact' to fill pauses and to gain time to think.
33. In conversation with others in English, I nod to show I am listening and interested; for example, I say 'Uhmm'.
34. If I am speaking and cannot think of the right expressions, I will use all-purpose words such as 'kind of' or 'something like'.

PART C

35. I look for opportunities to read as much as possible in English.
36. I look for people I can talk to in English.
37. I look for opportunities to write as much as possible in English.
38. I look for opportunities to listen to English as much as possible.
39. I notice my English mistakes and use that information to help me do better.
40. I notice the English mistakes of my friends and use that information to help me do better.
41. I try to find out how to be a better learner of English.
42. I plan what goals I am going to accomplish in learning English even when I do not have any test to take.
43. I arrange my physical environment to promote learning; for instance, I find a quiet, comfortable place to review such as the library.
44. I plan what I am going to accomplish in learning English in the long run.
45. I evaluate the general progress I have made in learning the language.
46. In order to remember new materials well, I often review, usually within three days or at most, a week.
47. I plan what goals I am going to accomplish in learning English in one or two months.
48. I arrange to study English intensively; for example, I just study English for a whole week

PART D

49. I encourage myself to speak English even when I am afraid of making a mistake.
50. I write down my feelings in a language learning diary.
51. I talk to someone else about how I feel when I am learning English.
52. I give myself a reward or treat when I do well in English.
53. If I do not understand, I ask the speaker to slow down, using phrases such as 'Could you speak more slowly?'.
54. If I do not understand, I ask the speaker to repeat, using phrases such as 'Sorry?', or 'I beg your pardon?'.
55. I ask other people to verify that I have understood or said something correctly, using phrases such as 'You mean ...'.

56. I practice English with other students.
57. I ask native English speakers for help.
58. In classes taught by native English speakers, I ask questions in English when I have questions.
59. In most classes, I ask questions in English or Japanese when I have questions.
60. I pay close attention to the thoughts and feelings of the people with whom I interact in the new language.
61. I try to learn about the culture of the place where English is spoken.

Appendix C: Background Questionnaire

1. Please print your student ID, your name, birth date, where you are from.
2. When did you start learning English?
3. What was the most enjoyable experience of learning English?
4. Have you ever studied abroad, or have you ever been to English-speaking countries? If you have, please write down your experiences in detail.
5. Do you have any English-speaking friends or neighbors around you?

Appendix D: Recruitment letter A

Initial recruitment letter

Volunteers Requested

April 1, 2002

Would you be willing to participate in a personality and language learning project?

I am looking for 100 adults presently taking an intermediate level English oral skills course at Doshisha Women's College. Participants must be willing to answer two kinds of questionnaires, and to offer the score of the TOEIC test you took at the beginning of the 2001 academic year. The project is called *Impacts of Extraversion/ Introversion and Associated Learner Strategies on Foreign Language Learning in a Japanese EFL setting.* I can offer you, upon completion of the research, a brief profile of your personality type and English learning, which may be helpful to improve your

English skills, and for your future career choice. This study will be done for my doctoral dissertation, which will be submitted to the Ontario Institute for Studies in Education of the University of Toronto (OISE/UT) in Canada.

The first questionnaire is about your ways of learning English, and the second one measures your personality type. They would be scheduled upon discussion with your course instructor xxxxx. All questionnaires will be scheduled outside of class hours. The TOEIC test score is necessary in order to observe the relationship between questionnaires and your English proficiency.

All information that you provide will be fully confidential. No information from this research will become known to anyone besides myself. I will ask you to provide a pseudonym instead of your real name, which will be used throughout the research. All the raw data gathered will be stored in a secure place. The data will be kept safely until I finish my dissertation. Upon completion of my dissertation, all paper materials will be destroyed by shredding and the computer files will be deleted.

I am interested in the ranges of influence of learners' personality type on English achievement, and in exploring learning strategies associated with personality type. The learning conditions in Japan are quite different from those in India or the Philippines, where English is used and recognized as a tool in everyday life. To improve English skills in Japan, we must inevitably find ways to learn English without the help of teachers outside the classroom. I would like to know how these strategies differ depending on a person's personality type.

If you are interested and willing to volunteer, please contact Natsumi Wakamoto at either the phone number or the e-mail address below. If you have any questions about the research, I would be happy to answer them. Thank you for your consideration of this request.

I look forward to your reply.

Natsumi Wakamoto
Ed.D candidate, OISE/UT
phone: 0774-65-8575
e-mail: nwakamot@dwc.doshisha.ac.jp

Appendix E : Recruitment letter B

Volunteers Requested
May 1, 2002

Would you be willing to participate in a personality and language learning project?

Among the participants of Phase-I of the project called *Impacts of Extraversion/ Introversion and Associated Learner Strategies on Foreign Language Learning in a Japanese EFL Setting,* I am looking for 40 adults presently taking an intermediate level English oral skills course at Doshisha Women's College. You must be willing to allow me to observe your class, to videotape the session, and to answer an open-ended questionnaire on the lesson.

The open-ended questionnaire is asking about what you were thinking or feeling during the class. I would like you to watch the video of the English lesson and answer the questions soon after the lesson. I would like to videotape the English lesson for that purpose. Further, I would like some of you to volunteer to be interviewed about the lesson, which will be audio-taped. This will be scheduled on another date.

I can offer you, upon completion of the research, a brief profile of your personality type and English learning, which may be helpful to improve your oral English skills, and for your future career choice. This study will be done for my doctoral dissertation, which will be submitted to the Ontario Institute for Studies in Education of the University of Toronto (OISE/UT) in Canada.

All information you provide will be fully confidential. No information from this research will become known to anyone besides myself, and my faculty adviser. I will ask you to provide a pseudonym instead of your real name, which will be used throughout the research. All the raw data gathered are stored in a secure place. The data will be kept safely until I finish my dissertation. Upon completion of my dissertation, paper materials and video tapes will be destroyed by shredding and the computer files will be deleted.

I am interested in the range of influences of learners' personality type on English achievement, and in exploring learning strategies associated with personality type. The learning conditions in Japan are quite different from those in India or Canada, where English is used and recognized as a tool in everyday life. To improve English skills in Japan, we must inevitably find ways to learn English without the help of

150

teachers outside the classroom. I would like to know how these strategies differ depending on a person's personality type.

If you are interested and willing to volunteer, please contact Natsumi Wakamoto at either the phone number or the e-mail address below. If you have any questions about the research, I would be happy to answer them. Thank you for your consideration of this request.

I look forward to your reply.

Natsumi Wakamoto
Ed.D candidate, OISE/UT
phone: 0774-65-8575
e-mail: nwakamot@dwc.doshisha.ac.jp

Appendix F: Task Type A

Listening to the interviews A (Actual task provided in Japanese)

Instructions:
This tape includes an interview with Lori about her new friend Mary. You are asked to write down as much information as you have understood in English. The length of the interview is about one minute and you have five minutes to listen to the tape.
1. During the five minutes, you can freely rewind, pause, or stop the tape to understand the interview.
2. During the five minutes, you can freely use the references on the table (bilingual, monolingual, and electronic dictionaries)

Lori's new friend Mary (Tape transcript)
Interviewer: Who's your newest friend?
Lori: Oh, gosh, my newest friend is uh is a wonderful woman that I met at the theater on line for the ladies' room. We were waiting an eternity, and we started to talk, and we both loved what we were seeing. And uh we just really hit it off, and we went out for coffee after the performance.
           We've gone to the movies several times. Uh, we've gone we've gone out for dinner. Uh ... We're planning to take a camping trip this summer together.
           We seem to have a lot in common, uh the things we like to do and the way we uh the way we live our lives. We're both um we're both hard workers, but we also like to travel, and we just seem to really hit it off. (133 words)

Appendix G: Task Type B

Listening to the Interviews B (Actual task provided in Japanese)

Instructions:
Karen, an English native speaker, will read an interview with Tom about his friend Erica. You are asked to write down as much information as you have understood in English. The length of the interview is about one minute and you have five minutes.
1. During the five minutes, you can freely say anything any time in English.
2. During the five minutes, you can freely use the references on the table (bilingual, monolingual, and electronic dictionaries)

Tom's new friend Erica (Tape transcript)
Interviewer: Who's your newest friend?
Tom: Yeah, we met at the at the job. We uh she got the we both got uh trained the same day, and got, you know, the job together and kind of helped each other through the training process, and that kind of was how we, you know, bonded.
            I like people who are funny, and she's just hysterical, and she was making me laugh all through the you know, it's the when I first met her she was making me laugh right away, and we just clicked, you know.
            We – we've been seeing a lot of each other lately. Um We've been going to the movies and stuff, and uh um we've been enjoying each other's company lately. (119 words)

Appendix H: Recruitment letter C

Third recruitment letter

Volunteers Requested

May 30, 2002

Would you be willing to participate in a personality and language learning project?

Among the participants of Phase-II of the project called *Impacts of Extraversion/ Introversion and Associated Learner Strategies on Foreign Language Learning in a*

Japanese EFL Setting, I am looking for several adults presently taking an intermediate level English oral skills course at Doshisha Women's College. You need to participate in the following listening sessions.

The five-minute listening (two) sessions where you will have a chance to listen to the tape recorder and to listen to a native English speaker's talk in person. I would like you to watch a video of the sessions and answer the questions soon after the session. The two sessions are scheduled on a separate date. I would like to videotape the sessions for that purpose.

I can offer you, upon completion of the research, a brief profile of your personality type and English learning, which may be helpful to improve your oral English skills, and for your future career choice. This study will be done for my doctoral dissertation, which will be submitted to the Ontario Institute for Studies in Education of the University of Toronto (OISE/UT) in Canada.

All information you provide will be fully confidential. No information from this research will become known to anyone besides myself, and my faculty adviser. I will ask you to provide a pseudonym instead of your real name, which will be used throughout the research. All the raw data gathered are stored in a secure place. The data will be kept safely until I finish my dissertation. Upon completion of my dissertation, paper materials and video tapes will be destroyed by shredding and the computer files will be deleted.

I am interested in the range of influences of learners' personality type on English achievement, and in exploring learning strategies associated with personality type. The learning conditions in Japan are quite different from those in India or Canada, where English is used and recognized as a tool in everyday life. To improve English skills in Japan, we must inevitably find ways to learn English without the help of teachers outside the classroom. I would like to know how these strategies differ depending on a person's personality type.

If you are interested and willing to volunteer, please contact Natsumi Wakamoto at either the phone number or the e-mail address below. If you have any questions about the research, I would be happy to answer them. Thank you for your consideration of this request.

I look forward to your reply.

Natsumi Wakamoto
Ed.D candidate, OISE/UT
phone: 0774-65-8575
e-mail: nwakamot@dwc.doshisha.ac.jp

Index

Linguistic Insights

Studies in Language and Communication

· · · · · · · · · · · · · · · · · · ·

This series aims to promote specialist language studies in the fields of linguistic theory and applied linguistics, by publishing volumes that focus on specific aspects of language use in one or several languages and provide valuable insights into language and communication research. A cross-disciplinary approach is favoured and most European languages are accepted.

The series includes two types of books:

- **Monographs** – featuring in-depth studies on special aspects of language theory, language analysis or language teaching.
- **Collected papers** – assembling papers from workshops, conferences or symposia.

Each volume of the series is subjected to a double peer-reviewing process.

Vol. 1 Maurizio Gotti & Marina Dossena (eds)
         Modality in Specialized Texts. Selected Papers of the 1st CERLIS Conference.
         421 pages. 2001. ISBN 3-906767-10-8. US-ISBN 0-8204-5340-4

Vol. 2 Giuseppina Cortese & Philip Riley (eds)
         Domain-specific English. Textual Practices across Communities
         and Classrooms.
         420 pages. 2002. ISBN 3-906768-98-8. US-ISBN 0-8204-5884-8

Vol. 3 Maurizio Gotti, Dorothee Heller & Marina Dossena (eds)
         Conflict and Negotiation in Specialized Texts. Selected Papers of
         the 2nd CERLIS Conference.
         470 pages. 2002. ISBN 3-906769-12-7. US-ISBN 0-8204-5887-2

Editorial address:

Prof. Maurizio Gotti   Università di Bergamo, Facoltà di Lingue e Letterature Straniere,
                       Via Salvecchio 19, 24129 Bergamo, Italy
                       Fax: 0039 035 2052789, E-Mail: m.gotti@unibg.it